THE
SUCCESSFUL
NETWORKER

EFFECTIVE STRATEGIES for UNNATURAL NETWORKERS

CHARLIE LAWSON

JAICO PUBLISHING HOUSE

Ahmedabad Bangalore Bhopal Bhubaneswar Chennai
Delhi Hyderabad Kolkata Lucknow Mumbai

Published by Jaico Publishing House
A-2 Jash Chambers, 7-A Sir Phirozshah Mehta Road
Fort, Mumbai - 400 001
jaicopub@jaicobooks.com
www.jaicobooks.com

Published in arrangement with
Panoma Press Ltd.
48 St. Vincent Drive, St. Albans
Hertfordshire AL1 5SJ, UK

To be sold only in India, Bangladesh, Bhutan,
Pakistan, Nepal, Sri Lanka and the Maldives.

THE SUCCESSFUL NETWORKER
ISBN 978-81-8495-797-6

First Jaico Impression: 2016

Printed by
Rashmi Graphics
#3, Amrutwel CHS Ltd., C.S. #50/74
Ganesh Galli, Lalbaug, Mumbai - 400 012
E-mail: rashmigraphics84@gmail.com

DEDICATION

To **Hannah**, **Alfie** and **MM**
Without you, it just wouldn't be worth it

x

I'D ALSO LIKE TO THANK:

Robin Schuckmann
There's no way this book would have been
written were it not for you

Anthea Lawson
You see, I can bang on too

Duncan Richardson
What a wonderful idea… I'm really not a natural
networker, am I?

Helena Clyne
You're a star

Andy Bounds
Just the best feedback and advice ever

The fantastic team at the BNI National Office
You all put up with me blocking out my diary to
get this book written, and being a bit stressed as
deadlines approached…

TESTIMONIALS

'I used to have an untidy desk.

So I asked tidy people what they did to keep things in order. But their advice didn't help. You see, tidying was so natural to them, they couldn't explain the steps an untidy person had to go through.

So I asked someone who used to be untidy what he'd done to become tidier. And he taught me the steps to take to change my habits. I haven't had an untidy desk since that day.

In the same way, most people who want to be better networkers ask natural networkers how to do it. But their advice doesn't always work. Because deep-down, natural networkers don't know the steps unnatural people need to take to change. Because they've never had to.

And that's why I love this book. Charlie Lawson clearly isn't a natural networker. He doesn't even like it much sometimes. But he's taught himself – and others – how to transform how they do it. You'll see the steps to take – many of which are annoyingly simple – to do so.

Best of all? It will change how you do things permanently. Now that is worth looking at!'

Andy Bounds,
winner of Britain's Sales Trainer of the Year

TESTIMONIALS

'With frank honesty, Charlie Lawson articulates what it means to face and conquer the innate reluctance and discomfort we all seem to encounter when it comes to 'putting ourselves out there' and mingling with strangers in order to reap the full rewards of networking for business or social advantage.

His sound, practical advice, highly effective yet simple strategies, and relaxed style will guide you step-by-step toward mastering the art of networking to achieve your greatest goals—an essential read for novice and seasoned business owners alike!'

**Ivan Misner, Ph.D.,
NY Times Bestselling Author and Founder of BNI**

•

'The most critical asset I have in my business is to be able to network. Online, Offline, no business can ignore it. Investing in these skills in large and small businesses is not an option. I strongly believe this should also be taught in schools. Charlie's book should be shared widely to ensure we create a global movement of networkers.'

**Penny Power OBE, Director & Founder –
Digital Youth Academy and Scredible**

TESTIMONIALS

'As an Unnatural Networker, Charlie is fantastic at explaining how to go about networking when it isn't something many business people enjoy. He has changed the attitudes and actions of many Unnatural Networkers at De Vere Venues, with great results and they are now Networking with a smile on their faces.'

Ian Conder, Sales Director at De Vere Venues

•

'I'm someone who appreciates the value of networking, and Charlie Lawson has a powerful message to help all business owners – whether running an established business or starting a new one – to utilise networking to its full potential.'

Jim Edgar, CEO Veritek Global

•

'An excellent introduction to networking for anyone feeling worried or uncomfortable about the topic. Charlie gives some great insights & actions for anyone keen to improve their networking skills.'

Jason Oakley, MD Commercial Banking, Metro Bank PLC

TESTIMONIALS

'Charlie's writing style is highly engaging, you feel he is having a conversation with you and appeals not just to your head but also your heart. His take on networking is very different to most: instead of being someone who has networked all their life, Charlie is someone that doesn't find networking easy, and has taught himself the hard way.

This book brilliantly articulates the learning curve that so many of us go through – which makes it wonderfully useable. Highly recommended.'

Paul McGee, (The SUMO Guy) International best-selling author and speaker

•

'Networking is such a fundamental part of business life and yet so many business owners fear it. My advice: read Charlie's excellent book that shows you how to not only get over that fear, but also generate real returns from networking.'

Heather Townsend, author of 'The FT Guide To Business Networking' and 'The Go-To Expert'

Foreword

I have known Charlie Lawson for nearly 20 years. In fact, I have known him since he was just a boy. Over the years, I have watched Charlie grow into a strong, gifted leader with highly developed, powerfully effective networking skills. For this reason, I was initially rather surprised by the title of this book – *The Unnatural Networker* – and even more surprised to learn that Charlie does not view himself as a natural networker. If you know Charlie, or if you meet him at some point even briefly, then you'll know exactly what I mean. Meeting Charlie, I might add, can be quite an experience for some. Why? Because Charlie is not simply a tall fellow – he is *towering*. He once shared with me that he's technically one inch below official giant status and I can easily believe it.

It's not just Charlie's physical stature that is striking, however. When it comes to networking, I think it's more than fair to say that Charlie is not unlike a giant among men in this realm also. As national director of BNI in the UK and Ireland, he is responsible for running the largest branch of the world's largest business networking organization outside of the United States. Thus, the experience and insight he possesses in regard to all aspects of networking is of an extremely rare caliber. Charlie's vast networking knowledge has been gleaned through years of training and real-world experience in discovering first-hand what leads to success and what, on the flipside, can be detrimental to any networker's chances of achieving growth and prosperity in the networking arena. His insights are truly unique and, in my opinion, invaluable to new networkers and seasoned networkers alike.

In fact, one of the things that strikes me about this book is how truly important people and their stories are to Charlie. He has always been interested not only in what others are doing, but also the story behind why they are doing it. The fact is, as individuals, our motivations for anything we do can be extremely diverse and they can greatly shape the way we each approach business. Charlie understands this completely and he has incisively tapped into this in a way that I find very refreshing.

The Unnatural Networker resonates with me on a significant array of different levels and I think the main reason behind this is that Charlie truly understands the insecurities the majority of business people feel but are often afraid to admit to, let alone address. He very clearly relates to and empathizes with the emotional rollercoaster which so many of us have endured as we've built our businesses. More importantly, through his courage and transparency in admitting that he hasn't always been too confident himself about networking and everything that goes with it, he allows us, the reader, to face a few core realizations and hard truths of our own, ultimately showing us how to turn these things to our advantage.

Whether you view yourself as a natural networker or not, *The Unnatural Networker* is a must-read as it is guaranteed to guide you towards ultimate business growth through highly effective networking strategies from a world-class networking expert. If your aim is to achieve any semblance of networking success, read this book, absorb the wisdom and insight it offers from cover to cover, and use what you learn. It will be an investment in your own growth which you will be forever grateful you made (though, be advised, as amazing as this book is, I'm afraid it still isn't capable of helping you grow to an inch below official giant height like its author – sorry).

Ivan Misner, Ph.D.
NY Times Bestselling Author and Founder of BNI

CONTENTS

PART 1

Introduction to
Networking

CHAPTER 1

What is an
Unnatural Networker?

I'm an Unnatural Networker

In July 2008, I attended an old school friend's wedding. David and I are part of a group of eight friends that have stayed in close contact. Today, now with wives and partners (and ever-increasing numbers of children), we've all remained close.

David's wedding to Lottie was on one of those amazing days when the British weather manages to do what it is supposed to do in summer. The venue was a stately home near Crewe, where every room, with the antique furniture, paintings and fittings, looked wonderful.

The regular wedding traditions were all there: after the wedding ceremony itself, all the guests were mingling and chatting on the lawn in front of the house, getting stuck into the Pimm's. Dinner was then served, followed by speeches, cutting the cake, the first dance, and of course lots more booze.

During the day, I noticed something. Whenever people were chatting, I only talked to my group of friends. For the wedding ceremony, I sat myself next to people I knew already.

When the guests went to sit down for dinner, the seating plan dictated that I would be next to people I knew well. OK, not my choice there, but it still suited me fine to not be next to strangers, and not to have to make uncomfortable small talk. As the evening progressed, the dance floor became busier and busier. I, with my two left feet, preferred to sit and chat with my friends.

Not once did I make the effort to go and speak to someone new, someone I didn't know, someone different. It's not exactly difficult to start up a conversation at a wedding. Everyone is (generally) happy to be there. There is a shared connection with literally every guest (i.e. we all knew David and Lottie). So I had the opportunity to meet new people, but I just didn't want to.

Why was this? I run a business networking organisation! I meet new people all day every day. I spend my entire professional time talking to people. What was the difference here? Indeed, at work I'll not only be meeting new people, I'll be up in front of them, speaking and training. So, not only do I spend a lot of time networking, I also train people how to network. Surely I should have no problem talking to people and socialising at a relaxed occasion like a wedding.

But the fact remains that I did have a problem with chatting to people at David and Lottie's wedding. I had no inclination whatsoever to put myself out of my comfort zone.

I must put this in further context by talking about my mum. Put simply, I don't know anyone who networks better than she does. I remember going to a funeral with her once, which was when it struck me just how good she is at engaging with other people.

The funeral was my great aunt's, who died when she was well into her 90s. Most of her generation had either passed away, or if they were still alive, were unable to travel to the funeral. So there were only a few people at the crematorium, and afterwards at the wake.

Now I know that this was a funeral, not a riotous party, but with so few people, there was virtually no conversation. Then my mum got going. Watching her in action was an absolute lesson. She got everyone chatting and enjoying themselves, as much as anyone is going to at a funeral. She talked to everyone. She showed a genuine interest in them. She introduced people to one another. She made the whole occasion… bearable.

Where was I in all this? Yes, you guessed it: I was cowering in the corner, trying to avoid talking to anyone. Or, when I got roped into a conversation by my mum, trying to appear to be vaguely interested.

So what is the relevance of these two non-work-related events? Why am I discussing them in a book about networking? Well, networking is talking to people. As will become abundantly clear over the course of this book, networking is about building relationships. The more you talk to people, the better the relationships you'll be able to build.

In a business context, we call it networking (and that word can be off-putting to lots of people). In social circumstances, we call it talking to people. In fact, it's exactly the same thing.

Both David and Lottie's wedding and my great aunt's funeral (and don't worry, we're not going to discuss another three weddings...) got me thinking. I started considering how I like to interact with people. I came to a conclusion. I don't really enjoy meeting new people very much!

It is true: I can categorically state that I, as the head of the UK and Ireland arm of the world's largest and most successful business referral and networking organisation, do not like networking! There, I've said it.

But why? Why is it that I am perfectly comfortable networking when I 'have to', but when I don't, it is the last thing I want to do? That is the question that has driven me to understand myself better professionally since I first asked it. It's the question that has led me to want to put down what I've learned in this book. I hope that others who feel the same about talking to other people can find the confidence within themselves to network.

You see, I'm not bad at networking. I know that in my professional life I'm very good at it. I can very easily enter a room of strangers, introduce myself, and get to know something about them. I know I can leave with follow up opportunities. I can also happily jump on stage and present how to grow a business through the power of networking.

It's just that for me, networking is not something that is naturally in my comfort zone. My natural preference and state of being is not to be out there, talking to everyone. I'm far happier sitting back, taking everything in, and spending my time with people I care about. But I can manage networking if I want to: it's just whether I want to or not. If I can persuade myself to take a step out of my comfort zone, I know I can network just as effectively as anyone else.

In essence, I'm an Unnatural Networker.

Networking is a learned skill

In business, we are told that we've got to network. Perhaps you're about to start your own business; in that situation what you need more than anything is for the phone to ring. Without clients, the new business will fail. If you already run a successful small business, you're probably looking for more new clients, or better new clients. This will allow you to grow the business and take it to the next level, or just to focus on the sort of clients you really want to work with.

You may work for someone else, but your role in the company requires you to bring in new business and generate sales. You may also be in the jobs market: either looking for something new, or these days, for any job at all. In each of these scenarios, we're told that networking is the answer. 'Go and get yourself out there in the market', we're told: and to be honest, that advice is right.

So, what do we do when we 'go and get ourselves out there in the market'? If networking is supposed to be so important, why am I hearing about the need to do it now, once I'm in the situation I'm in? Why wasn't I taught how to network when I was at school, college or university? I did a business degree at university. It included modules on strategy, accounting, marketing, customer service, but there wasn't a single word on networking!

According to the UCAS (University & College Admissions Service in the UK) website, there is not a single university or college course available anywhere in the country that focuses on networking (unless you're after computer/internet networking). Some institutions are starting to realise this, but it's only on a very small scale. My old school rang me up out of the blue recently and asked me to come and talk to 16/17-year-olds about how networking would help them in their career. But this is nothing compared to what's really needed.

I remember my teenage years very clearly. To be honest with you, my overriding concern right then wasn't so much how networking could help my career. Those were the days of being young, single, keen... and OK then, a bit awkward. They were the days of going to the pub or to parties, and trying to pluck up the courage to talk to members of the opposite sex! If only I'd known then what I know now about how to network, many of those conversations could have led to vastly different outcomes...

The point is that networking is a subject you can study. It is a topic you can read expert advice on, and it is a skill that, crucially, you can practise. There are many people, like myself, who just need a bit of help on who to approach when networking, and how to get into good conversations.

In this book, we'll look at how to:

- Approach people at a networking event

- Start conversations

- Keep conversations going

- End conversations

- Build relationships

- Follow up effectively

- Present yourself and your business effectively

- Use different types of networks, both face to face and online

- Come up with a networking strategy

In covering these points, this book will show you how I went from being a complete non-networker to an Unnatural Networker.

CHAPTER 2

What is Networking?

Working the room

So, do my experiences at the wedding and the funeral ring any bells with you? You'll probably fall into one of two camps. You may be thinking that there's no way you'd ever feel uncomfortable talking to other people at a social event, particularly where there is a strong common connection with the other people there.

The other option is that you're not very comfortable in these situations – a bit like me. You find it nerve-wracking when interacting with strangers and you'd far rather spend time with people you are comfortable with. In essence, meeting new people takes you out of your comfort zone. Let's look at that – there really is nothing to fear!

For a long time I believed that to be successful at networking you have to be able to 'work the room'. Working the room means that at any type of event you make sure you greet all the attendees. If it is a business networking event, that may also include swapping business cards with everybody there. When you leave the event, you will be sure that people will remember who you are and what you do. Politicians are regularly noted to be excellent at working the room.

Some years ago, I worked for a wine company in London, and a colleague of mine, Nicolla, was what I then perceived to be the ultimate networker. Essentially, she was excellent at working the room. Maybe the fact that the wine company's events involved wine had something to do with it, but I was always in awe of how easy Nicolla found it to chat to anyone and everyone at any event we were at.

Looking back, watching her in action was certainly a factor in my fear of networking. I thought that networking meant working the room.

Introverts and extroverts

In her book *Quiet: The power of introverts in a world that can't stop talking*, Susan Cain describes an extrovert as 'gregarious, alpha, comfortable in the spotlight… socializes in groups… the kind who's comfortable "putting himself out there"'. This is exactly what I perceived you had to be to be able to work the room.

I thought I needed to be absolutely confident to walk up to people, and not only introduce myself but be able to join in conversations. That might be with just one other person, or with three or four people. But it doesn't end there; new people will be brought into the conversation, and I'd move on to a different group of people.

So, as I started having to network myself, two key things held me back. Firstly, my only real example was watching Nicolla do her thing, confidently working the room. Secondly, I'd come to the conclusion that you had to be an extrovert to do this. How could the introverted me possibly be able to keep up with Nicolla and the like?

How do introverts look at the world? Susan Cain contends that introversion is about gathering information on a situation, and waiting before taking action. Instead of diving in confidently and gregariously, introverts will proceed cautiously.

Introverts don't look to engage with others at every opportunity. Introverts are more comfortable dealing with what they know about themselves. Clearly, there will always be shades of grey, but in general, apart from extreme cases of introversion, it doesn't mean that introverts won't interact with anyone. They'll just try to keep to themselves more, or look to mix with those that they are familiar with.

Once in a conversation, the introvert won't look to exit to find another person to talk to: as that would mean stepping out of their comfort zone again. Striking up the first conversation was hard enough after all!

Once in conversation, whoever they're talking to becomes someone they feel comfortable with. This often means that the conversation becomes deeper and less superficial. While the extrovert is off starting a new conversation to make sure they speak to everyone in the room, the introvert is really beginning to get to know the person they're talking to. This will take them far beyond the basic details of just finding out the person's name, what their business is, and where they are based.

Provided the introvert can effectively manage the conversation (and we'll discuss this in Chapter 6), they're going to find out lots of information about the person they are talking to. This allows them to become an even better networker than the extrovert.

It is worth knowing that somewhere between a third and half of the world's entire population are introverted. That means that when you go out networking, there is a good likelihood you'll be talking to an introvert. If you're feeling somewhat unnatural when it comes to your networking, there's a reasonable chance that whoever you're talking to will be feeling the same.

Extrovert / Introvert Case Study

Dr Ivan Misner, founder of the world's largest networking organisation, BNI, talks regularly about how he considered himself to be an extrovert. How could the head of a networking organisation, who is always talking to people and is commonly on stage speaking to huge audiences, not be an extrovert? But Ivan's wife, Beth, was convinced that Ivan is actually an introvert; in his own time, Ivan is much like me when it comes to interacting with other people. He'd rather keep his own company, or stick with people he knows already.

Ask Ivan now, and he's very comfortable describing himself as an introvert, but also a 'situational extrovert'. This means that when he needs to, he's able to turn on the extroverted elements of his nature to suit the situation he's in.

So what is networking?

To help me answer that question, I'd like to share a story with you that really helps to illustrate what networking *isn't* all about.

I was at an early morning networking meeting in Croydon recently, when I met an enthusiastic businessman who was promoting a combined fire and security protection system.

I'd not been there more than a couple of minutes when he approached me, shook my hand enthusiastically, and proceeded to hard sell his amazing new solution that would solve all of my domestic fire protection and security needs. Did I want to buy, at the amazing introductory price of £199.99, a saving of over 25% from the recommended retail price?

Er… no. Sorry mate, but would you please go away. He then moved on to the next person, giving them the same spiel. Did he sell any product to the people there that morning? Of course he didn't! You never know, his fire and security protection system might have been just what I needed, but his approach made sure I'll never find out.

There is a fundamental problem with going to a networking event trying to sell. Even if the buying process for your product/service is very simple, there's no paperwork to fill out, and the buyer has their credit card on them, you're still not going to sell anything.

Why? Because no one goes out networking to buy! Think about it: have you ever gone out networking with the intention of buying anything?

But at the vast majority of business networking events I attend, someone will try to sell to me. Even if they're not selling, they'll be thrusting their business card or brochure in my face, making me feel guilty if I don't take one. In times of economic difficulty, we're told that the best way to generate new business is by networking. Many of us put untold pressure on ourselves because we go out networking trying to make a sale or two. After all, we've all got to put food on the table.

However, this pressure to make sales drives people to become increasingly desperate in their attempts to sell. Yet they get no tangible results. This leads them to become worried about even bothering with going networking. Fears of it being a waste of time are realised, and the end result is no business being generated.

So what is networking then? The dictionary tells us that networking is 'a supportive system of sharing information and service among individuals and groups having a common interest'. Wikipedia states that networking is 'a socioeconomic activity by which groups of likeminded businesspeople recognise, create, or act upon business opportunities'. Sounds good – but for the Unnatural Networker like me, utterly useless.

I'd like to share what I believe networking to be, via an analogy originally presented to me by Andy Bounds, a communications guru I recommend very highly indeed.

He told me this about 10 years ago, but it created such a powerful visual image in my mind, and demonstrates so accurately what happens at a networking event, that I feel I should share it here.

Imagine a fishing boat out in the North Sea. The bulging fishing net is being hoisted out of the water, full of fish. As the net comes out of the sea, droplets of water cascade down the sides of the net. As they run down to the bottom of the net, they drip into a steaming hot cup of coffee.

You what? Stick with me on this one.

What does the fisherman expect to find in a bulging fishing net? Typically, three things: big fish, little fish, and the archetypal wellington boot. You'll find the same three things at a networking event. Let's take each in turn:

Big Fish: this is what the fisherman is really after: the big juicy fish that is going to sell for the most at the market. In a networking context, these are the people who you should go out looking for. Perhaps they are businesses with which you could strike up a strategic relationship, or they might be a great potential client. They are contacts who could really help move your business forward.

Little Fish: for every big fish, there will be a multitude of little fish which, while they are useful, just aren't as valuable as the big fish. Back at the networking event, they are people who may be able to help your business in some way, or they may just become contacts of yours. While useful, they won't move your business forward in a dramatic way.

Wellington Boots: for some reason, fishing nets always contain some rubbish. It could be a wellington boot, it could be an old tyre, or it could be a shopping trolley. Whatever, it is of absolutely no use to the fisherman at all. You'll definitely meet wellington boots when networking – trust me, there are a lot out there! They may be tripping over you to get to the buffet, boring you senseless with their life story, or perhaps encouraging you to buy their particular brand of widget with 25% off.

It's clear what the fisherman wants to find in his net: but how do you deal with the three types of people when networking? The wellington boots: move on quickly. The little fish: don't spend too long with them, because while useful to an extent, what you really need to be concentrating on is finding those big fish. We'll look at how to exit conversations (politely, of course) in Chapter 6.

How should you deal with a big fish? Well, to answer this, it's time to return to the final (and yes, I know, the strangest) part of Andy's fishing net analogy: the cup of coffee. There's no point trying to sell anything or finalise a strategic tie-up at a networking event itself: no one is there with that in mind.

Much better, especially with the big fish, is to start building a relationship. Then, as appropriate, arrange a time to meet for coffee at a later date when you can have a proper discussion.

Andy Bounds' fishing net analogy and the story of the hard selling fire/security system salesman in Croydon demonstrate two interesting points:

1. Networking isn't selling – it's about building relationships, and looking to set up a chance to meet on a one-to-one basis at a later date.

2. You'll meet people out networking who not only won't be of interest to you and your business, but who will actually damage your potential to achieve success through networking. Look out for those wellington boots!

Networking Extremes!

In Dr Ivan Misner, Mike Macedonio and Mike Garrison's excellent book *Truth or Delusion*, the authors ask a question that helps illustrate the relationship-building process perfectly. They ask whether you can network anywhere, anytime – even at a funeral. Clearly, the obvious response to that is, there's no way you can network at a funeral, how would the bereaved family feel?

But applying the logic of networking being about building relationships, and not about selling, and it is obvious that you absolutely can network at a funeral. If, when at a funeral, you meet someone and there are common interests between the two of you and your businesses, then should you stop talking to them, thinking 'No, I'm at a funeral, this is disrespectful'?

Absolutely not: at the event itself, you'd just focus the conversation on getting to know them. Building a relationship. Afterwards, you can arrange to meet over a coffee, at which point you can take the relationship further and, if appropriate, actually do business.

The point here is not whether you should network at a funeral. What I'm saying is that you can network anywhere, anytime, because networking doesn't actually involve doing business. Networking is just the building relationships part – the business comes later.

Forget who is in the room!

So, we now know that networking isn't about selling. However, I've lost count of the number of times I've heard someone say: 'There's no one at this networking meeting that I could do business with'. Unfortunately, they are missing one of the golden rules of networking: the people in the room aren't the ones that matter.

You'll no doubt have heard the phrase: 'It's not what you know, it's who you know.'

Well, in networking, there's more to it than 'who you know'. Instead it's about who you know, how well you know them, *who they know*, and whether they are willing to introduce you.

We'll come on to talking about introductions in Chapter 3, but first let's look at who we know. It's amazing how many people you do know when you think about it. Consider this spider diagram:

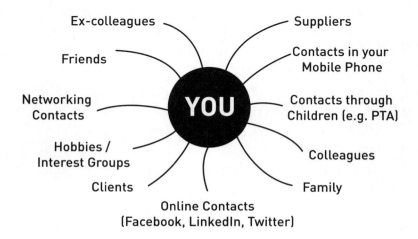

Try totalling up the number of people. The chances are, if you've been around for a little while, you'll know many hundreds, or even thousands of people.

In BNI, we reckon that, on average, each of our members has 1,000 contacts. That's not to say, of course, that we'll speak to all of our contacts every day, every month, or even every year. However, we can define contacts as people who would take your call given a bit of background on where you know them from.

So, let's say the networking meeting that you're at has, aside from you, 40 people in attendance. It is fair to assume that they'll all have similar contact networks to you.

Therefore, the potential isn't just the 40 people in the room. Instead, those 40 people could connect you with up to 40,000 people. That's when networking gets interesting.

As an Unnatural Networker, it's worth remembering this. If you're ever tempted to pass up on the chance to network because you are feeling a bit nervous about it, or you've heard there are only going to be a few people there, you just never know who those people are going to know. And with 1,000 contacts each, that's a lot of people.

Chapter 2 Action Points

- Have a think where you are on the Introvert – Extrovert scale. Ask yourself honestly if your networking experiences in the past have been tainted by where you sit.

- Make a firm commitment to yourself to NEVER try to sell any products or services at a networking event.

- Start thinking about who would be a big fish for you. You might define them by a job category, or you may need to focus on specific people.

- Once you know who your big fish is, consider what the best way to build a relationship with them would be.

- Take a piece of paper, and draw the contacts spider diagram for yourself. How many contacts do you think you have?

CHAPTER 3

Referrals

What's a referral?

So we now know what networking is. Let's move on to a key issue: making networking worthwhile. In Chapter 1, we talked about why we go out networking: perhaps it's to bring in new clients, or to grow the business. Maybe your boss has sent you networking.

Whichever it is, it is vital that you show some sort of return on your time invested in networking. That return, by the way, can't just be a stack of business cards! We're in business and we need to look at this in terms of the financial return.

To get a financial return, we need to be finding new clients. These new clients often won't be people you meet at a networking event. As we've just seen, the people in the room are just the tip of the iceberg; it's the people they know that we want to get introductions to.

In networking terms, we call getting introduced to people 'referrals'.

A referral is an introduction to someone who is in the market for your product or service, and crucially, they are expecting your call. It won't necessarily lead to business; you've still got to go and sell yourself as to any other potential new client.

But the key part about a referral is the fact that the third party has been warmed up, so they are keen to talk to you and hear what you have to offer.

As an Unnatural Networker, knowing that someone will definitely take your call and is looking forward to it certainly makes it easier to be confident about speaking to them.

Why are referrals so good?

I heard a fascinating story recently at a dinner party that perfectly illustrates why. I met a friend of a friend who runs a decorating business, and his frustration was obvious as he was enduring a slow start to the year – the phone had just stopped ringing.

I asked him what he was doing to promote his business. He'd printed several thousand leaflets and dropped them through letterboxes all around his local area. I asked him how many calls he'd received. From all that effort, he'd received just one call to quote! However, as it happened, that one call had been for what would be a very good job: repainting an entire five-bedroom house.

As you can imagine, he was desperate to get the work. When the client called back to discuss his quote, they told him that they'd ruled out four other companies, and he was on a shortlist of two. They told him they would think about it over the weekend, and call back on Monday.

He told me he spent a nerve-wracking weekend waiting, but was very confident about winning the pitch. He'd been super-professional, arrived early, provided guarantees about the quality of his work, was available to start immediately, and the clincher in his mind: he personally was an expert in painting ornamental fireplaces (of which there were two in the house).

I have to say I very much identified with the decorator: we've all been in situations like this. Maybe we're perhaps pitching for work, perhaps going for a job, but we know that we're the right person. We just KNOW it.

Monday morning came, and the client phoned. They'd decided to choose the other company! The decorator, despite being absolutely gutted, did what every good businessman should do in this situation, and asked for feedback from the (non-) client.

"Was I professional – do you think I could have done the job?" "Absolutely," came the reply.

"Was I competitive on price?" "Definitely." In fact, his quote had been cheaper than the other company's.

"Well then, why didn't I get the job?" "Because the other company came from a referral."

Referral Business is Better

From all points of view, referral business is better than that gained through other means:

- For the **business supplier**, referrals tend to be easier to close, and have fewer objections. Referrals often bring customers with a stronger sense of loyalty that remain clients longer.

- For the **referrer**, they increase their credibility with both the end user and the business.

- For the **end user**, the trust element is crucial. Why take a risk with someone from an online search?

How long will it take me to get referrals?

A fair question.

The short answer is 'as long as it takes to build trust'. Trust is the vital element in a referral, particularly for the referrer. They're the one in the middle; if the service provider (the receiver of the referral) does a bad job, then the referrer risks damaging their reputation with their contact (the person needing the service).

Picture your best friend. Now imagine that it is 4.30am, and they are calling you. Would you take the call? You would, wouldn't you? Why? Well, because you have a good relationship with them, you want to help them.

Networking is very similar: although don't worry, it doesn't involve middle of the night phone calls... When we build up relationships with people, we just want to help them. Whether it's helping their business in some way, or recommending them, we want to help.

However, we need to be realistic. If you think that you can walk into a networking event and come out with business, it's not going to happen. Building relationships takes time. Networking is not a quick fix for an ailing business.

Here are two different methods to understand the time it takes to build relationships. In a moment, we'll come on to something called the Referral Confidence Curve. Firstly though, we're going to look at the VCP process.

Visibility, Credibility, Profitability

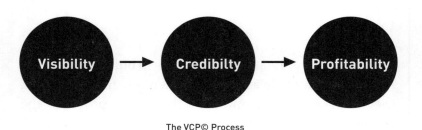

The VCP© Process

Visibility – This is when we first meet someone, and get to know them. For example, at a networking event, you might spot a particular attendee on the guest list, and get introduced to them.

Immediately, you'll both be forming an impression of each other: how are you dressed, what's your handshake like, are you a nice person to talk to, do you look them in the eye? You may already have found out about the person by looking at their website, or their online profiles.

As conversation develops, you'll find out fairly quickly whether you might be able to do some business, or if you might be able to help each other. At this point, you may agree to meet for coffee the next day. The visibility process continues at this one-to-one meeting, as we find out more about each other's business.

However, we can't yet generate referral business from or for this person. To do that, we need to move on to the next stage: Credibility.

Credibility – This is the stage where we find out if the networking contact is any good. Continuing our example, it will start at the one-to-one meeting, but may well require many more contacts and touch points between the pair of you before credibility is achieved.

If we're going to refer business to anyone, then there's one thing that will have to be achieved before we can do so: we need to trust the person. If I'm going to refer someone I know, perhaps my client who's paying my mortgage and feeding my kids, I need to trust them completely.

I need to KNOW that my networking contact is going to do a good job. I can't take the risk with my reputation. Credibility is where we get that trust from: perhaps we see examples of their work, we could try them out on a small job, or we might hear testimonials about their work from other clients.

Profitability – Once we've gained credibility with our networking colleague, we can move on to the final stage: Profitability. Now that we know, like and trust the person, we can pass referrals between us that help both of us grow our business.

The VCP process outlines the overall journey to networking profitability. But I think we can delve even deeper into how long it will take to get a referral, and as we're about to see, it depends on what you do.

The Referral Confidence Curve

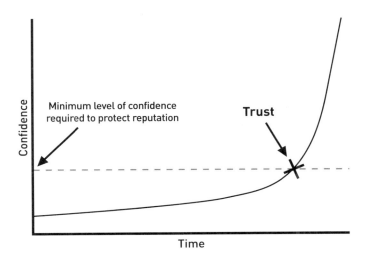

Take a look at the Referral Confidence Curve. On the horizontal axis, you have time. On the vertical axis, there is confidence. What we mean here is the amount of confidence a potential passer of a referral needs to have in you and your business. There will be a certain level required in order to protect their reputation, as shown by the dotted line.

The Referral Confidence Curve always starts slowly, keeps moving slowly, and then suddenly shoots up. The point at which it does so is as soon as it crosses the confidence required line. This point is where trust has developed.

So, back to the time axis. How long does it take to reach the point of trust? That depends on the industry you're in.

Let's take a couple of examples:

1. A Florist

Imagine you're a florist (if you are a florist, no need to imagine…). How are your networking contacts going to know you're any good? What sort of risk are people taking in trying out your services? Obviously, the answer is very little: they'll buy a bunch of flowers and find out the quality, value and service of your offering straightaway. The point of trust is relatively easy to reach.

2. A Financial Advisor

Now imagine you are a financial advisor. How will your networking contacts know if you're any good? What sort of risk will they be taking in trying out your services? Clearly, it's a much greater risk. If they are going to try you out for, say, their pension requirements, they'll need to provide personal and financial information. If you did a bad job, they'd be risking not only their own future but also their entire family's. The point of trust therefore takes much longer to reach.

To get referrals, you have to be trusted by your networking contacts. There are plenty of other professionals just like the financial advisor where people can't just try out your service to generate trust. It is the quality of relationships that you build that will make the difference; how much are you prepared to help your networking contacts?

So let's look at a great way to build relationships through the types of referrals you give.

Not all referrals are the same

We've talked about a referral being an opportunity to present your business to a third party, where that person is looking forward to your call. However, within that definition there are different types of referrals. As the diagram suggests, we call them Reactor / Promoter / Creator.

- You are a **Reactor**. This means that when you hear people asking for help with a problem, you react by offering someone in your network. As an example, you might hear a client say: 'We're having a bit of a nightmare with our office supplies company. They used to be OK, but they've become really unreliable. Can you recommend anyone good?'

  This is a very easy way of passing referrals. However, from the point of view of your office supplies contact who wants to generate business, they are relying on someone asking. This doesn't happen every day.

- You are a **Promoter**. This means that you interpret what people are saying to you to help your contacts get business. Sticking with our office supplies analogy, you might have heard your client complaining: 'This office supplies company, they've sent the wrong order again!'

  At this point, you could jump in and say: 'Would you like an introduction to a good office supplies company? I know a particularly good one, who would definitely be more reliable than your existing supplier.'

  Promoting differs from creating in that your client hasn't explicitly asked for an office supplies company. But in complaining about their existing one, they are, in effect, asking for help. The challenge, again from the point of view of your office supplies contact, is that you are still relying on hearing the frustrations of your client.

- You are a **Creator**. This means that you proactively go out of your way to help people get the opportunities they are after.

  Here's a real story of how I helped Tim, an office supplies contact of mine. Tim really wanted to get in touch with the facilities manager at the school near to our office. He asked me if I could help, which I was keen to do as he was a good contact of mine.

  Unfortunately, though, I didn't know anyone in the school, so I had to think outside the box to help. Tim had been able to get hold of the name of the facilities manager, so I rang the school and asked to speak to him. This is what I said:

"Hello, my name is Charlie Lawson, you don't know me, but I'm trying to help a contact of mine…" I then proceeded to tell him about Tim, and how he'd saved another school £2,000 a year on their stationery supplies.

I was slightly surprised at just how easy it was to gain agreement from the facilities manager to accept a call from my contact. But it really was that easy. The pair met, and guess what? The school changed its stationery supplier.

Why was my cold call so different from most others? I believe that because I had no vested interest in the business deal, and made that clear, I called with the impression of doing the school a favour. This dramatically changed the whole tone of the cold call, such that it became a 'warm call'.

So, here's a question for you. If you could only have one of these types of referrals, which would you go for? I'd have the creator referrals; that's where the most value comes from, because the recipient hopefully gets access to their preferred (and possibly dream) referral.

I'd also argue that if I am prepared to create on your behalf, I'll have no problem promoting and reacting. If I'm only prepared to react for you, it's a much bigger leap to move towards promoting and creating.

How do you get people creating for you? Very simple: create for them. If you keep helping other people, at some point they are going to ask you how they can help you in return. In BNI, we call this Givers Gain.

Givers Gain is the founding philosophy of BNI. It means that if I can pass business to you, you will pass business back to me in return. It is based on the principle of what goes around, comes around. Givers Gain doesn't usually work in direct terms; if I pass a referral to you, I'm not going to expect a referral straight back from you the next time I see you. However, I can expect something back from the group as a whole.

A great way of looking at Givers Gain is to think of attending a party where everyone brings a bottle. If you were to turn up without a bottle, how would you feel? If you were to turn up to lots of parties, consistently never bringing a bottle with you, what would everyone else think about you?

Chapter 3 Action Points

- Think about some of the clients you've worked with recently. How did you meet them? There's a good chance many will have come from referrals: *but you didn't think about them in that way!*

- Of all of your contacts, consider with whom you have a profitable networking relationship. Whatever the number, set yourself a goal for how many new profitable networking relationships you'd like.

- Work out how many of your contacts you are at the point of trust with.

- Think through your contacts, and ask yourself if any of them are referral creators for you.

- Pick someone in business that you know well, and determine that you will find a referral for them.

CHAPTER 4

Where can I Network?

So, you've made a decision to go out and network! You've psyched yourself up, and attempted to get the butterflies in your stomach to lie down and have a rest. The question now is: where do I go to network? Let's look at that now.

I remember very clearly a conversation I had at a Chamber of Commerce networking event in south-east London some years ago. The guy I was talking to was a solicitor, and he was telling me that at virtually every networking event he went to, he only ever met other solicitors. This was no good to him: why would he want to just talk to other people in the same industry?

There is value in meeting people who do what you do, as we'll see shortly, but I had to laugh to myself. Every time I'd been to that Chamber meeting, there was a group of three or four people from his legal firm who always spent the entire event chatting to each other. I'd just happened to catch him as he made his way back to his colleagues having visited the buffet table.

It's no wonder he only met other solicitors if he never strayed from talking to people in his own company; they might just as well have chatted around the water cooler in the office!

We'll look at who to talk to while at the networking event in Chapter 6, but the point illustrated by the solicitor is a valid one. Who you're likely to meet when networking is vital to help you decide which network you should consider getting involved in. So to help with this process, here is a run-down of some of the types of networking that are available.

Casual contact networks

Casual contact networks offer you the chance to meet lots of different people from a wide range of professions and backgrounds. Typically, they will hold a regular monthly meeting, often over lunch. The reason they are called 'casual' networks is that attendance at the events is very much on a casual or relaxed basis. For example:

- Attendees will come and go as they please

- There is no requirement to attend at all, so there may be any number of people in attendance on a particular day

- There will be a random mix of professions/attendees

- You may well meet people who do the same as you

Sometimes, there will be a short speaking session from the sponsor of the event, or from one of the members on a relevant business topic. Other than that, there is no particular meeting agenda. The aim is for the participants to network in an open format.

The Chamber of Commerce is a great example of a casual contact network. The Chamber is a worldwide organisation, and across the UK they have 53 geographic specific groups. For more information, visit their website at: www.britishchambers.org.uk.

By their very nature, casual contact groups are, well, quite casual, so they aren't necessarily the place to generate huge amounts of business. However, the groups are an excellent place to go and make new contacts. As with many things in life, the more you put into the network, the more you'll get out.

Strong contact networks

Strong contact networks will have only one person per profession in the group, so you have an effective monopoly within the group in your line of business. Strong contact groups are run with only one real purpose: to generate business opportunities for the members. Where casual contact groups operate under a loose structure, strong contact groups involve a lot more commitment. Some examples of this commitment are:

- The group meets regularly; plenty of strong contact networks meet weekly. The more often you meet with your networking contacts, the better the relationships that will be developed.

- The group will expect you to attend. If you're not there, you can't give/receive business, or hear what other people are looking for.

- The group will expect you to bring business or new contacts to the table. Again, the more you put in, the more you'll get out, so if you forget to attend each week, or don't try to help the other members, it will be very obvious. So they'll stop passing business to you...

In addition, strong contact networks will tend to follow a very structured meeting agenda. This will include (but isn't limited to):

- Open networking (very much like casual contact networking)

- A short presentation, often 60 seconds, by each of the attendees on their business

- A longer presentation (10 minutes or so) by one of the members so they can go into more detail on their business

- A business passing session, where members of the group pass business referrals to each other

BNI is the best example of a strong contact network. All over the world, BNI sets up 'chapters' of professionals where there is only ever one person per profession in the group, and they meet with the prime reason of looking for business opportunities for one another. BNI chapters operate under the principle of Givers Gain: by giving business opportunities to others, you will get business in return.

BNI tracks the business passed through its 'Thank You For The Business' system, so when you visit a chapter, ask about the amount of business that the group has generated. That way, you'll get a realistic idea of the amount of business you could potentially receive (provided you participate in the system!). For more information on BNI, visit www.bni.co.uk (UK) or www.bni.ie (Ireland).

Strong contact groups exist to generate business opportunities. If getting more business is top of your priorities, then strong contact groups are a good place to start. Not only will you make new contacts, you'll get a support network around you that, provided you look after them, will look after you.

Industry specific networking

Industry specific networking, usually organised by professional associations within specific industries, exist to provide networking within a sector. Given that the majority of attendees will be from the same profession, the meetings are less about generating business; instead, they will largely be about exchanging ideas and education (and usually gossip) within the industry.

Examples of professional associations include:

- Association of Chartered Certified Accountants (ACCA)

- Royal Institute of Chartered Surveyors (RICS)

- Chartered Institute of Marketing (CIM)

- British Psychological Society (BPS)

- Royal College of General Practitioners (RCGP)

- Institute of Chartered Secretaries and Administrators (ICSA)

- Federation of Master Builders (FMB)

To become a member of a professional association, you obviously need to be a professional in the trade or industry that the association specialises in. If you are, and you'd like to practise some of the networking tips in this book in a 'friendly' environment, then an industry specific networking event may be a great place to start. There won't be so many chances to generate new business, but there will definitely be opportunities to build up your confidence in talking to people. You'll also learn a lot and keep up to date with the latest trends in your industry.

Could you attend a professional association meeting if the attendees are your target market? There are two options to consider here:

a. Look for professional associations that offer an associate membership. This will have fewer benefits than full membership, but may allow you to network with the members. Beware though: your competitors may well have had the same idea! The members may not appreciate (what they perceive as) being sold to at their event.

b. A better option is to get invited along to the professional association networking event by one of their members. For this to happen, you will clearly need to have built a good relationship with your inviter. If you can make this work, though, that person can be an introducer for you, and break down some of the barriers you may otherwise encounter.

It is really important to understand the culture of the group of people you're going to network with. This means: What is the group like? How do they do things? What do they wear? If everyone is expected to wear a suit and tie, and you turn up in an open-neck shirt:, how will you go down? It's likely that before you've even started, you'll have damaged your credibility. The best way to get round this is to ask in advance.

Community service clubs

Community service clubs offer a chance to network with other business people, with the emphasis on putting something back into the community. The clubs don't tend to be aimed so much at networking specifically, but over time and through helping the community projects that the club focuses on, relationships inevitably build.

These relationships tend to develop into friendships, and once friendships are in place, it is easy to see how business opportunities can develop.

Rotary is one of the most well-known service clubs. Rotary is an association of local clubs that come together across the world under the umbrella of Rotary International. Their aim is very much to promote community through a passion for service. As Rotary quote on their website: 'We are 1.2 million neighbours, friends, and community leaders who come together to create positive, lasting change in our communities and around the world.' You can find out more about Rotary via their website: www.rotary.org.

Women only networking

There has been an increase in the number of women only networking groups over the last few years. Clearly, as a man, I'm not going to be able to offer you great personal insight into women only networking...

However, some insights from women I know who have attended women only groups are that groups tend to be:

- More casual than strong contact networking groups.

- Filled with members who are dedicated to helping each other achieve success. This doesn't necessarily mean members try to refer business to each other. More often, members are simply keen to use each other's services wherever possible.

- Very keen to help members promote themselves as professional businesswomen, and many members say they pick up plenty of business tips.

Some women say they are uncomfortable with networking in groups that are dominated by men (and because many business sectors are still dominated by men, so, unfortunately, are many networking groups). The opportunity to network with other women provides a welcome respite and a mutually supportive environment.

Social organisations

It is often thought that networking is only about business; however that isn't true. One of the best ways to build relationships is through areas of common interest. Frequently, these areas can be social, sporting, religious, family, hobby-based: anything.

The relationships that develop through these groups of friends and contacts also provide opportunities to share business. Indeed, within particular interest areas, groups are starting up that recognise the value of networking, thus allowing attendees to mix business with pleasure.

Whatever interests you have, there's likely to be a local group or umbrella organisation that supports that activity. Go along, offer to help, get to know people; over time, relationships will build. You never know what connections might come out of it.

Online networking

Online networking is exactly what it says on the tin. People often differentiate social media from all of the face to face networks above, claiming that they are entirely different. But really, it's all just about building relationships, whether you do it online or in person.

We'll cover online networking in much more detail in Chapter 12, but for the moment, here is a quick look at three of the most commonly used social networks:

- **Facebook** – Facebook has become a global phenomenon since being set up by Mark Zuckerberg in a college bedroom in the US in 2004. It has expanded into the biggest social network in the world, with over a billion users. It has increasingly become an important way for businesses to interact with potential clients.

- **LinkedIn** – LinkedIn is the world's primary professional business social network. Where

Facebook was started off as a strictly social tool and has since developed in other directions, LinkedIn was always conceived as a platform for business. All users on the site are business professionals, with many of them in decision-making positions within their organisation.

- **Twitter** – Twitter is a micro-blogging site, in which short messages ('tweets') of up to 140 characters are sent out by users to be read by their 'followers'. Twitter states that over 500 million tweets are sent daily by 200 million users (figures correct at the time of writing).

Whichever platform you choose to network online, one of the key benefits is that you are able to build up visibility quickly, measured in terms of the number of people who are interested in what you're saying. Each platform has a slightly different word for this: on Facebook, you'll have Friends, whereas on LinkedIn you count the number of Connections you have. On Twitter meanwhile, look out for your number of Followers.

Online searches are very easy to do; by finding information relevant to your industry, sharing it with your contacts, and through the process of blogging, online networking enables you to position yourself as an expert within your field. It is a great way to find people and build your credibility at the same time.

Choosing the best network for you

So, that's just a quick rundown of the various networking options available. To get a full picture, checking them out yourself is an important step. This book will certainly get you prepared for what you'll find.

But I can give you some guidance, and there are pros and cons to each network. Some will be better for generating business, others will be better for building long-term friendships.

You also need to bear in mind how much time you are going to spend networking. If you network too much, when will you do any actual work? Also, if you do network in lots of different places, I'd question how much you are going to be able to commit to each one. It's about finding a balance.

My advice to the Unnatural Networker is that it is best to pick more than one network, so you can try different approaches. However, don't go overboard and try to network everywhere! Good networking practice would be to choose two or three different networks and commit to them fully. Remember, the more you put in, the more you're going to get out in return.

As an Unnatural Networker, look for places where you can build your networking confidence. I'm not sure that service clubs or social clubs would be the best place to start; both of these are about building relationships over the very long term, and perhaps don't have the necessary focus to help you gain confidence quickly.

Given that you can come and go as you please, casual networking groups are a great place to practise your networking skills; you just won't see a great return in terms of business generated.

You'll need to decide whether women only networking groups are for you; clearly, for half the population, that decision has already been made for you, and you can't go! For women though, they can offer a potentially less threatening place to start your networking.

Similarly on the 'safe' front is industry specific networking. While business generation is lower on the list of priorities, the chance to pick up information relevant to your industry and practise your networking with friendly people can be invaluable.

Online networking is certainly worth investing time in. There's no doubt that in the 21st century, if your business hasn't got a good online presence, you'll be missing out. It's just so easy to build up a wide following. It also has the distinct benefits that you don't have to leave the house, and you can carry on your networking while on the move.

I firmly believe strong contact networks offer the most to the Unnatural Networker. By getting into a structure where you go networking on a weekly or regular basis, you will learn very quickly how to network effectively.

Networking groups definitely offer you the best chance of making contacts that will lead to new business. Because there's a requirement to turn up and actively bring business or contacts to the group, you know that the members there will help you, provided you're prepared to help them.

My tip: My recommendation is to pick two or three networks and participate in them actively. Go for a networking group, and combine it with a strong presence on one of the online networks.

That's two: this may be enough – but if you're going for a third, just pick the one that you feel suits you best.

Chapter 4 Action Points

- Do some research into your networking options. Is there a Chamber of Commerce meeting locally soon? Is there a networking group near you? Does your industry have a professional association that organises events? Is there a local community organisation/project you could get involved with?

- List your current activities, both interests and work-related. How much networking are you already doing?

- Decide which (up to three) networks you're going to participate in.

- Book to attend one, and put the date in your diary!

- Set up a profile on one of the main online networks (or refocus your existing profile if necessary).

PART 2

Get Out There and
Network!

So, you've decided you're going to go out and network.
Not only that, you've worked out where you're going to go and network. What next? We need to make sure that you're all set for the networking event you're going to attend.

In Chapter 5, we'll get ready to network, before looking at two distinctive types of networking.

In Chapter 6, we'll look at attending big networking events, where the key thing is to get into good conversations. To some people, notably extroverts, the notion that we should spend an entire chapter on how to have a conversation would be crazy. To others – you Unnatural Networkers out there – there is a huge amount to think about.

Then, in Chapter 7, we'll look at networking on a far more intimate scale: one-to-one.

CHAPTER 5

Before you go Networking

In many situations, being prepared makes a difference; how is it that when you're on time and prepared for an appointment, there's no traffic on the road and you get there early? Leave for the appointment late, with last-minute preparation to do before the meeting starts, and there will be traffic jams everywhere, making you more frustrated as well as horribly late. There are usually knock-on effects on how well the meeting goes, too.

You don't want to be dealing with all this when you go to your first networking session. As an Unnatural Networker, just the experience of going will take you out of your comfort zone.

It certainly did for me; I can still remember the first networking event that I went to. It was an early morning breakfast meeting, at a golf club nearby. It was early February, so it was cold, frosty and very dark as I drove there. I parked my car, turned the engine off, and then I just sat in the driver's seat, trying to distract myself from what I was about to do and think about something else.

After two or three minutes, I got out of the car and kept saying to myself: What am I doing, what am I doing, what am I doing? I so nearly turned round and drove off, but after what seemed like an age, I opened the door to the golf club. I was so nervous.

The point I'm making here is that you'll have enough on your mind already. If you haven't prepared for the experience, then it will only make it worse, and decrease the likelihood of getting results from your networking. As the saying goes, if you fail to prepare, prepare to fail!

So, here are four items that are worth preparing before going out networking:

Preparation Item 1: Set goals

This isn't the place to go into detail on goal setting as a topic:, but if businesses (and individuals of course) don't set goals, there is a dramatically reduced chance of achieving success.

It's the same when it comes to networking. To make attending the event worthwhile, it is vital to think carefully about what you want to get out of it. Setting goals makes it easier for the Unnatural Networker to enjoy a successful and worthwhile networking experience.

So, what goals can you set? Here are four possible goals:

	At this Networking Event, I will aim to:
Goal 1	Close 5 new pieces of business
Goal 2	Arrange 5 follow up meetings with people I meet
Goal 3	Make some new contacts
Goal 4	Meet 5 new people

Which of those do you think is the best goal? Well, hopefully you'll have spotted the deliberate error: as we saw in Chapter 2, there is no point trying to close business at a networking event, since no one is there to buy. So goal No. 1 is out.

What about goal No. 2? That seems like a reasonable goal to set, doesn't it? Well yes, from the point of view that having a follow up meeting afterwards is a sensible aim: but it is important to insert a touch of realism here.

The delegate list (more on that in a moment) will give us an idea of who will be in attendance, and of course you never know who you're going to meet. But can we really be sure that we will meet five people with whom it would be worth having a follow up meeting? It just may not happen.

This takes control of the situation away from you, and through no fault of your own, you would miss your target. That doesn't help the confidence of the Unnatural Networker!

What about goal No. 3? That would fail the first of the criteria that make up SMART (Specific / Measurable / Achievable / Relevant / Timely) goals. 'Making some new contacts' is in no way specific.

By process of elimination then, goal No. 4 is definitely the best. It is:

- Specific – it is clear what you want to achieve

- Measurable – easy to measure: have you met five new people yet?

- Achievable – it is certainly achievable; of course, your goal may be higher

- Relevant – the point of attending the event is to meet new people, so yes

- Timely – needs to be achieved by the end of the event

I used to think that a goal like No. 4 seemed too simplistic and a waste of time. However, as an Unnatural Networker, I've found it provides a key advantage.

I've noticed that it gets me going to networking events where otherwise I might not have gone. It is very tempting to think something along the lines of *Oh, this event is unlikely to gain me anything,* but just setting a goal of making a number of new contacts makes it much easier for the meeting to be a success. And that makes it easier to walk in the door to start with.

It also gives me the right expectations of what should realistically be achieved from going along.

Preparation Item 2: Look at the delegate list

Depending on the event, you will often receive a list of all those attending prior to the event. Sometimes this will be by email a day or a week beforehand. Sometimes you will be given the delegate list on entry to the event itself. You may even have to request it.

Whichever it is, spending a bit of time preparing can help you get a lot more out of the networking event. If done well, it will also help with your goal setting that we've already discussed.

The delegate list will typically show people's name, company name, and their profession. It may also provide contact details, although this won't always be the case as it makes it very easy for attendees to 'spam' people after the event. We'll look at this in Chapter 11 when we discuss follow up.

However, armed with the information of who is there and what they do, you can plan and prioritise who you'd like to meet.

So, for example, if accountants are useful contacts for you, then you can scan down the list, make a note of all the accountants, and then set a goal to meet some or all of them when you're at the event (as per goal setting above). If there's a certain individual that you've heard of and would particularly like to meet, they can be at the top of your list.

If you are only given the delegate list on the way into the networking event itself, it's still worth doing some preparation. Instead of just attacking the room and talking to the first person you see, spend a few minutes by the door or cloakroom, and look through the list. It may feel like this small time investment is wasting or cutting into your networking time, but it is well worth it if it means that you are focused on speaking to the right people.

Preparation Item 3: What to wear

Now this might appear to be a non-issue for some but, believe me, for others it's a very important question. Two of the most common fears I hear from Unnatural Networkers are: 'Networking is just full of people in suits', and 'My normal working work clothes are jeans and a polo shirt – I'd feel very uncomfortable being the only person dressed like that'.

There's a very simple answer to this. You should absolutely go and network in the attire that is suitable for your trade or profession. If that means a suit, that's fine. If it means jeans and a polo shirt, that's also fine. Think about it: if a painter and decorator dresses up in a suit and tie, is that congruent with their business? Similarly if an accountant or solicitor dresses down and doesn't wear a suit, how do they come across?

I remember a particular member of BNI who was in a chapter some years ago. He was a financial advisor who ran a very successful business. He was a very authoritative person who presented himself well – both in how he dressed (suit, tie, etc.) and how he spoke to a room of people.

As such, he was the chapter director of the group, which meant he ran the weekly meeting of the group. His chapter was doing really well, and in turn he was getting a huge amount of business from it. Then, one day, I received a call from someone in the chapter saying that things in the group weren't going so well. Having not attended for a while, I went along to have a look.

The member who had called me was absolutely right. The whole group seemed to have lost some of its professionalism. Nothing too overt: some of the presentations weren't very good, one or two people turned up late to the meeting, and there was a bit of chattering when someone was presenting their business.

But then it dawned on me why. The financial advisor was running the meeting wearing a short-sleeved open-neck shirt, and shorts. His short sleeves revealed a couple of tattoos. Now I don't have anything against tattoos! It's just that in certain professional contexts, they are best covered up.

I talked to him afterwards, and he told me that business hadn't been great recently. When I questioned him on his attire, he said that he'd gone for a change of image so that he came across as more friendly and approachable. He simply hadn't made the connection between being a financial advisor and the need to dress appropriately.

In this case, though, it wasn't just the financial advisor suffering. It was affecting his whole networking group, because as the director, they took his lead. So they reduced their professionalism, affecting all of their businesses.

It wasn't hard to turn around the fortunes of the group after that.

The point here then is to dress congruently for your business. As a tradesperson, though, it's best to avoid wearing the clothes that you'd actually wear on a job itself: how would you like to meet someone in a paint/grease/cement-stained shirt?

So clean, smart and professional is the best way to go, and the great thing about this for all of us Unnatural Networkers is that is what we'd probably be wearing anyway. Easy!

Standing out from the crowd

I went to an all-day networking event recently for 400 or so people, which included lots of networking time, as well as speaking sessions from top business experts. In the mid-morning coffee break, I met a man who was dressed in full chef's whites, including a tall chef's hat.

He was dressed like that because he ran a catering business, and he found that it was a great conversation starter. I couldn't help but agree! Not only that, he found he made more contacts, and ultimately got more business from his networking when dressed like that.

His outfit was all the more striking when we were sitting down in the session immediately afterwards. I was near the back of the room on the right, and it was easy to see the caterer sitting near the front on the far side of the room. He really stood out!

Preparation Item 4: Make sure you've got your networking tools with you

So, what do we need to make sure we've got with us when preparing to go networking? Here are some of the things you should think about:

1. **Business cards**: this one sounds obvious: never go out networking without them! It is much easier to arrange a follow up meeting with an interesting contact if you both have your business cards with you.

2. **Pen**: perhaps not so obvious this one, but crucial nonetheless. In many ways, it comes down to how good your memory is. If you can remember every detail you hear, then fine, but I certainly can't! Much better to have a pen to write down the odd note of what actions may be required.

For example, let's say that you achieve your goal of making five new contacts. Now, assume that one of those five was one of the really big fish we discussed in Chapter 2.

When you and the big fish were in conversation, you both agreed that you'd meet up for coffee, but the onus was on you to call the other person and set it up. I know that if I didn't make a brief note about this at the time, I would look at the five cards after the event and think *Now which one was it that I was supposed to call?* I just wouldn't take the risk.

3. **Mobile phone**: as technology improves, it becomes easier and easier to carry everything around with us. Because most of us have smartphones these days, having our phone means we've also got our contacts list, our emails, and plenty of other applications that can help us when networking.

Your mobile phone is worth having with you for a couple of reasons. Firstly, it may well be your form of taking notes. Secondly, and we're getting into more advanced networking territory here, having your contacts with you allows you to make connections for people while networking. If this makes you feel distinctly like an Unnatural Networker, rest easy, we'll look into this in more detail when we look at one-to-one networking in Chapter 7.

4. **Collateral material**: this should be labelled as 'optional', and really depends on where you're going to network. Some events will have a place for attendees to place brochures, leaflets and the like; in which case, why wouldn't you bring some materials to further promote your business?

Other networking events don't have this facility, and you'll spend the whole time there juggling your various bits of information with your business cards, while you shake people's hands and try not to drop your cup of coffee. In this case, make life easy, and don't bother with the leaflets or anything else. The best thing to do is ask the event organiser how their event runs, and then you can be well prepared.

5. **Smile**: now, I appreciate that this one isn't something you can pack into your bag, but it is absolutely crucial to success at a networking event. Who wants to talk to a miserable so-and-so who doesn't smile? The energy and enthusiasm that you will project to the people you come across when you smile will pay dividends.

6. **Badge**: you will often receive one on the door as you enter a networking event, or in some cases, such as being part of a networking group, you'll be given one as part of your membership. Whichever it is, trust me when I say this – from one Unnatural Networker to another – a badge is the single most useful tool you have to help make networking a more comfortable experience. We'll discuss this in more detail in Chapter 6, but for the moment just remember the golden rule: never go networking without a name badge!

Chapter 5 Action Points

- Set a goal of the number of people you want to meet at the event you're going to.

- Study the delegate list (or ask for it if you haven't received it), and decide which big fish you'd like to meet.

- Work out what you'll wear to the event.

- Gather your materials: business cards, pen, collateral, badge. Create a badge that prominently shows your first name.

- Smile! Even if you have to fake it...

CHAPTER 6

Interesting Conversations

So it's time to go and network. It's time to meet some people. This really means just one thing: it's all about conversations. If you want to take the next step on the networking journey, you've got to be talking to people.

Body language

Picture the scene. You, the Unnatural Networker, have just walked through the door into a busy networking event.

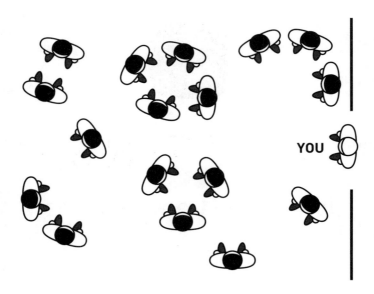

You've got yourself a cup of coffee and in front of you is a large room, with lots of people busy networking. There is a general buzz from the room: everyone looks busy, and like they know exactly what they're doing, right?

Wrong! They might all look like they know what they're doing, but plenty will feel just like you do. They certainly did when they walked through the same door a few minutes earlier.

Where to start? The key here is to break the room down, and work out who to talk to by looking at people's body language. Human beings betray a huge amount of detail about themselves through their body language, and it is no different in a networking context.

Have a look at these typical thoughts from people at a networking event:

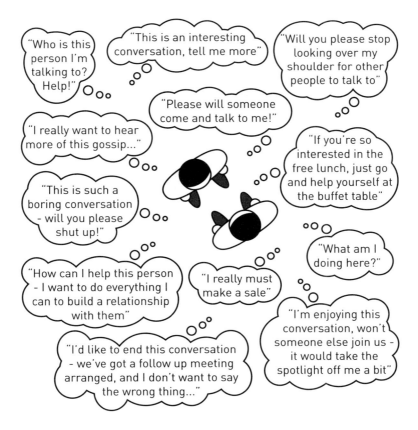

For each of these scenarios (and trust me, you'll see all of them), the person's body language will give plenty of clues as to what they're thinking. If someone is gossiping, having a personal conversation, or – dare I say it – trying to make a sale, then closed body language will be appropriate. The people talking will be putting up a barrier that says 'don't interrupt us'.

For many of the others, it is human nature to present a more open body language. When trying to escape a conversation, or looking for others to join in, the way we stand will reflect this.

So what do we mean by being closed?

Closed twos and threes

These diagrams demonstrate closed body language, in both a two and a three. By closed, we mean:

- They are looking at each other head on

- They are close together

- Their heads may be bowed slightly

- There's little chance of interrupting

- They may even be sitting down

- If there is a lot of background noise, they may be talking very close to each other's ears

Sometimes you'll even see a closed four. Often, when you do, they will be a group of four people who came to the event together (or maybe even work together every day!), and by staying in the closed group, it makes them more comfortable.

As an Unnatural Networker, this may even have a certain appeal, but it won't get you very far in terms of results. The best conversations can be had when there are only two of you involved.

Not Networking!

It is even possible to get really big closed groups of maybe eight or ten people. Typically, this will happen in a smaller overall networking event, where everyone is a bit unsure about what should be happening. One louder and more confident person will hold court over everyone else. However, given there's no chance of anyone building a relationship with another, this cannot be described as networking.

Let's compare what we've seen so far with closed body language to what being open is like.

Open twos and threes

In these diagrams you can see an open two and an open three. This is the best body language formation to look out for as an Unnatural Networker. What do we mean by 'open' in this context?

- The couple are side by side

- They typically (and this increases in open threes and fours) create a V-shaped formation

- They are definitely talking to each other, and maintaining eye contact, but are aware of the room around them

- They are respecting each other's personal space

Going back to the original overall room, it now becomes clearer what we're dealing with. No one could contemplate the prospect of tackling the whole room in one go. It is much better to break down the mass of people into the individual open/closed twos, threes and fours.

Have a look at the big networking scene again; it is easy now to make out the small individual conversations going on.

All we need to look out for are open body language conversations. Don't even bother trying to talk to people demonstrating closed body language. They are subconsciously telling you 'don't interrupt me!' At the same time, those keeping themselves open are trying to tell you that they would welcome you coming to talk to them. So don't fear it, go for it!

The best groups to go for are open twos. It is just easier and less nerve-wracking to go up to two people than it is three or four. However, don't discount threes and fours. If their body language is open, then we know that they don't mind us coming into their conversation. However, it would take a very confident approach to just stroll right into the middle of an open four, and say 'Hi everyone, I'm Charlie…'!

The better, more considerate approach is to start at the end of the line, and work your way into the conversation. When this happens, it is common to see the three or four break up into smaller conversations in twos and threes. This is inevitable: it is virtually impossible to build a relationship with someone unless you get to talk to them one-to-one.

There is one other type that it is worth looking out for as an Unnatural Networker. From my list of thoughts on Page X, there were a couple (*What am I doing here?* and *Will someone come and talk to me please?*) which likely indicate that the person is themselves an Unnatural Networker. They may not be in a group with others, might be lurking near the coffee table, and are on their own looking for people to talk to.

Why not talk to these people? Firstly, it makes it nice and easy for you to get into a conversation. But secondly and perhaps more importantly, how will the other party feel now that you've struck up a conversation with them? You talking to them is a genuine act of kindness (never mind that you were both in the same boat), and they will warm to you.

They won't necessarily become your best client ever, but relationship-building has to start somewhere. Why not make the first move?

But what do I actually say?

As a fellow Unnatural Networker, I can almost hear your thoughts being shouted at me. So you're telling me I've got to go networking – I accept that. I've just about made my peace with the fact that I'm going to have to talk to people, and I can kind of see how the body language section that we've just been looking at does make a lot of sense. But what the hell am I actually going to say?! Without doubt, this has always been the hardest bit for me.

Well, much like the rest of this book, the answer is hardly rocket science:

- Hello, I'm Charlie*, how do you do?

*You may want to avoid using my name at this point, unless of course you are a fellow Charlie, in which case you have a great name…

- Hi there, how are you doing?

- Hello, my name is Charlie. What's your name?

- Hello, my name is Charlie – who are you?

- Hello, nice to meet you, I'm Charlie.

- Hi there, I'm Charlie – what do you do?

Like I said, hardly rocket science. I hope you weren't expecting more! All of these phrases are really just simple conversation starters. All of us, Unnatural Networkers or not, will have used them time and again.

So if there's no problem with any of these conversation openers, why is it still a challenge? The nerves simply come from being Unnatural Networkers, uncomfortable with the situation. It can't be about what we are actually going to say!

Let's just remind ourselves of a couple of key facts: firstly, the only point of networking is to build relationships. You're not there to hard sell to these people!

Secondly, as we've already seen, provided you pay attention to people's body language, and look for welcoming, open features, you can be certain that whoever you approach will be interested in talking to you. They are at a networking event after all.

We can take this a stage further with a few other options to open a conversation when networking. Bear with me if the first one sounds a bit corny:

- Hi, do you come here often?

Yes, it's the most clichéd chat-up line in the English language – but, joking apart, I'd like to make a couple of observations. Firstly, there really are a lot of similarities between networking and chatting people up. Both require you to talk to people, both are about building relationships, and long-term success in both tends to come from not rushing into making the 'sale' straightaway...

Secondly, there's a reason why 'Do you come here often?' is one of the most well-known chat-up lines: it works... or at least as far as getting you into a conversation. And it will work in a networking context, because it gets you talking.

Here are a few others to consider:

- It's my first time here – do you mind if I join you?

- Do you mind if I listen in? I don't know anybody here.

- Do you mind if I join in your conversation?

These three are particularly useful when joining in an existing conversation, whether it's an open two, three or four. The one that I have used more than any other is the last one: Do you mind if I join in your conversation? It says a number of things about you. Firstly, you're polite and considerate (i.e. you are not going to just come in and start dominating). Secondly, you're interested in what the other people are saying.

Lastly, it probably reveals just a little about you being an Unnatural Networker. By demonstrating your vulnerability, you come across as unthreatening. This allows people to take you under their wing and feel good about doing so. This all helps with relationship-building.

Bear in mind that these phrases are ones that I've tended to use when I'm networking. It is really important to be yourself; if you wouldn't use the words here, don't! Say whatever comes naturally to you, and say it in your own style. That way, however nervous you may be, the real you will come across. Since relationships are the end goal, that is really important.

Please come and talk to me!

As an Unnatural Networker, you can teach yourself to look out for body language, and with practice it gets easier. But it would be easier if you didn't have to make the first move the whole time.

Well, I have good news! It is perfectly possible to get people to come up to you. But there is one condition: you have to wear a clearly named and visible name badge.

This is a very common fear amongst Unnatural Networkers, and one that I vividly remember myself. From 'it will ruin my look', through 'I won't be told to do anything', to 'everyone will stare at me', there are a multitude of excuses that I've heard over time to avoid wearing a name badge.

Imagine that you're at a networking event, and consider the following two introductions:

"Er, um, hello, my name is Charlie, who are you?"

"Hello Bob, my name is Charlie – what do you do?"

In life, it is great to look for win-win situations, where both parties in a situation feel good. Take the first introduction: it would be a win for the other person, because someone has come and talked to them. But how would you as the Unnatural Networker feel about using that phrase? For me, even now with lots of practice, it requires me to pluck up my courage. For the beginner, it's almost a non-starter. Definitely not a win-win.

Take the second phrase. A win for me: sure, as long as I can read his badge, then I know that I can't go wrong with this opener. It is a good confident start that sets me up in conversation. For Bob? Definitely a win. Firstly, someone has started talking to him. Secondly, and perhaps more importantly, I've also asked him what he does. The conversation is right where he wants it to be.

Wear a name badge, and you increase the chance of people coming up to you and talking to you. Don't wear one: you never know, your next best client (or access to them) may just walk right past you at a networking event, too shy to risk introducing themselves.

This also brings us on to an important point. Given that we've been talking about going networking for the first time, we have overlooked the likelihood of seeing people you've met before. You're often going to see people you've seen before!

Regardless of me being an Unnatural Networker, I'm terrible at remembering names. I always have been. Unfortunately, given my position in BNI, people tend to recognise me, and this can cause some interesting challenges.

'Hi Charlie', someone will say when we meet at an event or function.

'Hi, how are you?' will be my slightly stumbled, embarrassed reply. Now I KNOW that I've met the person before. I don't have a problem remembering faces, but with names, like I said, I'm terrible!

If they are wearing a name badge though, a quick glance down and the reply is a much more satisfactory 'Hi Tim, how are you...?' This isn't about it being better for me (although less embarrassing maybe); I really want my networking contact to feel respected and that I'm interested in him.

After all, it is the relationship between us that will determine whether the two of us are profitable networking partners.

Badge-tastic

1.
Your name badge only NEEDS to include your first name. It is a conversation starter. Of course, there's no harm including your surname too, but it's our first name that is the most important.

2.
It's also useful to state your profession. This will make it easier to get into a conversation about what you specifically do.

3.
Do we really need your company name / email / phone number?

It's a conversation starter, nothing else - lose the business card!

4.
Make your badge professional looking - print it big and bold. This way people will spot your badge from several feet away, and come and make contact when they're looking to engage in a new conversation.

5.
Wherever possible, wear your name badge on the right hand side, as high up as you can. When you're networking, and meet someone for the first time that's wearing a name badge, mentally pause when you shake hands.

If you're wearing your badge on your left, it will be out of the person's eye line, putting them back in the situation where they can only ask who you are. Wear it on the right, and shake hands, you'll find your badge is directly in their view, making good communication easy.

Brilliant first impressions

So you're now ready to actually speak to people. 'But what if the other person doesn't want to talk to me?' 'What if they don't care about what I do for a living?' Both are commonly asked questions of the Unnatural Networker.

This little story from a recent networking event I was at illustrates this challenge well. When I was there, I met a guy called Mark. Here is a transcript of our conversation:

Me: "Hello there Mark, I'm Charlie – what do you do?"

Mark: "I'm an accountant."

Me: "Oh."

At that point, the conversation ended. Now, don't get me wrong:, I wasn't trying to offend him (or every other accountant reading this). I just couldn't think of anything else to say!

Compare that scenario to this one – from a similar event – where I got talking to a lady called Anne. Anne was about 4'11" and (I'm guessing here) was somewhere in her late 50s/early 60s.

Me: "Hello there Anne, I'm Charlie, what do you do?"

Anne: "I'm a weightlifter."

Me: "What? Really? Tell me more!"

I couldn't believe my ears! How on earth was this tiny person a weightlifter? It didn't make any sense, so I had to ask her for more about what she did.

So Anne told me that her business was stress counselling. She helped her clients lift weight off their shoulders. We had a very interesting conversation about her business, which left me in no doubt as to what sort of clients would help her grow her business.

Comparing Mark's and Anne's responses then, the following points strike me:

- Mark's response was very inward focused: telling me what HIS role is.

- Anne's response made me think immediately about the benefits her clients get. In other words, it was focused externally.

- Mark left me struggling to think of another question to ask.

- Anne got me to say 'tell me more' which meant we had a proper conversation.

Many potential networking conversations never happen because of scenarios like the one with Mark the accountant. The key, then, is to introduce yourself in a way that gets the response 'tell me more'. To do this, consider the following points:

1. Think about what your customer gets AFTER they've used your product or service. Do you, for example: save them money, keep them out of jail, make them more efficient, add to their bottom line, help them retire earlier?

2. Avoid using your own job title – that's about you, not your customer. No one really cares about the flashy title you have within your organisation.

3. Wherever possible, use 'interesting' words. For example, as an accountant, do you help people pay less tax, or do you SLASH their tax bill?

4. Don't make your introduction long-winded. This is a short introduction, designed to get a conversation started. I once met someone from a solar heating company at a networking event, and his introduction was: "We install solar systems for both commercial and domestic markets. A quality installation assures you of superior performance, fitted to maximise efficiency for your central heating or just for your hot water needs." Or at least I think it was. I'd lost the will to live after the first sentence…

We always hear that first impressions count. Not only that, but depending on which bit of research you read, you have between five and 30 seconds to make that first impression. It is no different in networking: we all make judgments about the people we meet. It may be your dress sense, your hair, your hygiene, your business card, or what you say. You can vouch for the fact that people will judge you.

As an Unnatural Networker, I don't want to scare you. But it's better to be prepared. And when it comes to starting conversations, it is no different. Having a good introduction for yourself will pay dividends in networking results, and ensure you don't miss opportunities to create great new contacts.

Keeping conversations going

So we've plucked up the courage to go and talk to people, and not only that, we've delivered an interesting first line to get the conversation off the ground. Unfortunately though, this won't generate a return on our networking investment. As we've said many times now, the goal of networking is to build relationships. If we break off our freshly started conversation immediately, we're not going to get very far.

So we need to keep conversations going, and there is just one simple key to this: you've got to make the conversation interesting.

It's very simple. All you have to do is start by talking about the other person. Think about it. Who are you most happy and confident talking about? You! The answer is the same for literally everyone else on earth. We all find it dead easy to talk about ourselves.

The conversation is much more likely to continue if the other person thinks the conversation is interesting. They will think it's interesting if they get to talk about themselves.

There is another benefit to talking about the other person: it means that at some point the conversation ought to come round to what you do. If they don't ask about you after a while, it will give you a good idea about the sort of relationship you might be likely to build with them.

Andy Bounds, the noted expert on communications and sales, talks about 'winning the YOU game': you win if you talk about the other person first. Andy's point, very much like the principle of 'What goes around, comes around', is that it's polite to let other people go first. It will help build better and quicker relationships, but you also know that your turn is coming up.

Therefore, all we have to do is find ways to talk about the other person. How do we do this? By asking the following 'W' questions: Who? What? Where? When? and Why? interspersed with How?

Here are some examples:

- **Who** are you?

- **What** do you do?

- **Where** are you based?

- **Where** do you cover geographically?

- **When** did you start doing what you do?

- **Why** do you do what you do?

- **How** did you get into what you do?

- **What** are the latest trends in your industry?

- **What** excites you about what you do?

- **When** did you start going networking?

- **Who** is a good contact for you to meet?

- **Why** would you be interested in making contacts with *accountants*?

- **How** do you help your clients?

Don't worry! You are never going to need every single one of these questions. There will be plenty of others you could ask as well. But as you ask these types of questions, the conversation will develop. It may be that the first question you ask allows the conversation to flow, or it may be the fifth question.

Having a stock of simple Who/What/When/Where/Why/How questions makes it so much easier. Remember: we only need to keep the conversation interesting for a little while. The vast majority of people you meet networking are going to want to find out about you at some point.

Incidentally, you may have noticed that one or two of the questions towards the end of the list above start to move away from basic knowledge about the person you're talking to. These are the sorts of questions to ask when we're getting more focused on generating business for our networking contacts.

These will come up again when we discuss one-to-ones in Chapter 7. We'll also discover another useful tactic for having interesting conversations when we look at storytelling in Chapter 8.

Business cards

It's now time to talk about business cards. As we mentioned in Chapter 5, business cards are a vital tool to have with you. However, it is important to use them in the right way.

There are plenty of people who go to networking events just to hand out as many business cards as possible. But how much of a relationship are you going to build by forcefully handing out stacks of cards? If cards are unwanted and you can't remember who gave them to you, there is a far greater chance that they will just end up in the bin.

Much better practice is to wait until you are asked for your card. This means the person you're talking to actually wants your card. Of course, this doesn't always happen, so if you'd like to make sure someone asks for your card, the best way to make this happen is to ask for THEIR card. Once they have given it to you, it isn't a problem to offer your card to them.

Remember the fishing net analogy? The whole point of going to a networking event is to look for the big fish, and aim for a cup of coffee. Once the two of you have established that there would be a mutual interest in meeting up, this is the ideal time to swap business cards. When you do so, you can confirm the next step. Perhaps you'll email or call the next day to set up a one-to-one meeting, or maybe you agree you're going to meet next Tuesday.

What if you've forgotten your business cards? This is very frustrating when a) I've met someone who is a good potential contact for me, and b) they've shown enough interest in me to want to ask for my card so they can follow up.

Of course, you're thinking *I never forget my business cards when I'm out networking*. Think again! These scenarios typically don't arise at a networking function; at an event, we tend to be prepared, and carry a stock of business cards with us. More likely, this will be a chance encounter: perhaps on a golf course, or while dropping the kids off at school.

So, what to do? Well, here are two solutions to make sure that this potential golden opportunity doesn't go awry:

1. If you've forgotten your business cards write your contact details on the back of one of their business cards.

2. If they don't have any business cards with them, ask them to give you their phone number or email address. Once you've noted them down, agree a time to call or email them. This way, the follow up steps are agreed before you've even stopped talking. As we'll see in Chapter 11, if networking is to generate any real results, it HAS to involve follow up.

Exiting conversations

As an Unnatural Networker, it can be very tempting to stay talking to the same person once we've started a conversation. Trust me on this, I've been there. Once you're in a conversation, and you've started to build a relationship, to wrench yourself out of it and have to start the process all over again can feel very painful.

However, you may remember that we set ourselves the goal of meeting five new contacts. Equally, we don't want to monopolise the other person's time. They've got their own networking goals to hit as well. So it's one down, four to go.

You may also actively want to get out of the conversation. Yes, I'm talking about the wellington boots from our fishing net analogy. You will meet people with whom you have absolutely no connection whatsoever; perhaps you found them really boring because they only talked about themselves, or perhaps there just wasn't a connection between the two of you that's worth pursuing. Whichever it is, you'll still need to leave the conversation.

So, how do you exit conversations? It's very simple. Consider the following phrase:

'It was lovely meeting you.'

Say that, while shaking hands, and what are you telling the person? Your wording is very clear – it WAS nice to meet you – i.e. goodbye! That is without doubt the best way to exit a conversation. It's definite, but very polite. However, there are other options that can provide even more of a win-win.

You may remember that one of the good 'W' questions we discussed was 'Who is a good contact for you to meet?' This question, or rather the answer to it, provides you with your salvation.

Let's say, for example, that when you asked that question, the person said that solicitors are a good source of business for them. Well, when you want to end the conversation, simply look out for a solicitor who's attending the event, and make an introduction.

The win-win comes because you get to end the conversation, but more importantly, the other person gets to talk to someone of interest to them. You never know where that conversation might lead, and you will have played a crucial role in setting it up.

If nothing else, the person you didn't want to carry on talking to doesn't feel like you cut them out, they feel like you tried to help them. All good relationship-building. What if you can't see a solicitor nearby, or you don't know everyone in the room? Just ask the person you know best if they know a solicitor.

Even if they don't, you've broken the initial conversation, so it will be easy now to follow the 'it was lovely meeting you' route. Even though you haven't succeeded in putting the other person together with a solicitor, they will surely have been pleased that you tried.

The best networking tip I have ever heard

Hopefully, through the course of reading this chapter, you will be able to see that having conversations at a networking event is simple. That doesn't mean it won't take you out of your comfort zone. Remember, I'm an Unnatural Networker just like you, I've been there, and I still feel it whenever I go networking.

To finish this section, here's a great tip. I heard this early on in my networking career, and it really works. The tip is to think about the networking event as though it were a party at your own house.

When you host a party, your primary concern is that everyone who comes has a good time. You'll be welcoming them to your home, making sure everyone has a drink or food, and introducing people to each other. After all, you know everyone there, so you're able to make this happen.

When attending a party as a guest, you tend to be more reactive to what's happening around you. You'll wait for other people to come and talk to you, or wait to be offered a drink. Think about that the next time you go to a networking event. Even if you aren't the host, try acting like a host instead of as a guest. You'll be amazed at the difference it can make.

Chapter 6 Action Points

- Next time you attend a networking event, before you talk to anyone, spend a few moments studying body language. Look for open twos, closed threes and so on. Then go and introduce yourself!

- Wear your badge, high up on the right side if at all possible.

- Come up with your interesting first line to introduce yourself. Are you a printer, or do you make people look good between the sheets?

- Mentally prepare a stock of Who/What/When/Where/Why/How questions, ready to keep good conversations going.

- Try to win the You game: remember, in a conversation, you've got to talk about the other person first.

- With a friend, practise exiting conversations with 'It was lovely meeting you'. It will then feel more natural when doing it for real…

CHAPTER 7

One-to-One Meetings

It's all networking...

Have a look through the following list of scenarios and decide which situations you would describe as 'networking':

- Having coffee with a friend

- Having dinner with a group of friends

- Chatting with colleagues at the coffee machine in the office

- Having a few drinks in the pub with a client

What did you think? These don't sound like typical networking situations, do they?

However, for me, it's not whether the scenarios could be described as networking. Better to ask whether these situations give you a chance to build relationships. The answer to that is an unqualified yes.

So given that building relationships IS networking, all these scenarios can be described as networking. Traditionally, many people's view of networking is limited to the sort of mixer events that we discussed in Chapter 6. Networking comes in all shapes and sizes.

So in this chapter we're going to talk about interacting with a much smaller number: just one person. We're about to see that one-to-one meetings offer the very best chance to build relationships. One-to-ones are the most powerful way of networking.

The True Power of One-to-Ones

Let me tell you a story to illustrate why I believe one-to-ones to be so important in the relationship-building process. The story is about a guy called Steve. Steve is a great networker – a web designer – whom I've known for a number of years.

I had regularly heard Steve ask for a particular referral, and every day, on my route to the office, I pass by the premises of the company he was interested in getting into. Every time I drove past, I always thought to myself I really must try and help Steve out with that referral.

But I never did.

Then, one day, Steve and I were having a one-to-one over a coffee. We'd been talking for about an hour about his business, which clients he was currently working with, who he was looking to do business with, and so on. Of course, as I knew already, he was still looking for an introduction to the company he'd mentioned before.

Then, as the meeting was starting to draw to a close, Steve and I got into a conversation about Formula 1 racing. Neither of us knew that the other was into F1, but we had a discussion about our favourite drivers, races we'd been to, and so on.

How we got on to the subject is irrelevant but the effect of that conversation was profound.

I immediately felt I knew Steve that much better. This was despite the fact that I already saw him fairly regularly, I had heard him talk about his business many times before, and had just spent another hour getting to know him even more.

Now I knew 'stuff' about him. Crucially, that stuff helped me build a rapport with him. I now had a deeper connection with him that I didn't have before, and that connection, although I didn't realise it at the time, was going to help me find him a referral.

The next time I drove past the premises of his dream referral, I didn't just think to myself 'Oh, I really must try and help Steve'. Instead, I pulled over, went in and introduced myself, and got him a referral. It certainly hadn't been planned, but as I drove along and saw the company's sign, I just went for it.

Following our conversation about F1, how I felt about Steve changed. So much so that I was prepared to go out of my way to help him.

The only difference was that we had simply found out some 'stuff' about each other.

The power of one-to-ones

Let's take a look at a few reasons why one-to-ones are so powerful:

1. One-to-ones are a chance to go much deeper into the person you're talking to. At a large networking event, there is never much time to talk, so it is hard to find out a great deal about someone.

2. Another key challenge exists at a networking event compared to a one-to-one meeting: there are other people there! Other attendees means interruptions, both good and bad. That doesn't happen in a one-to-one.

3. In a one-to-one meeting, you know that you've got the undivided attention of your partner for the allotted time of your meeting. At a networking event, whoever you're talking to will have their own goals and aspirations of what they want to get out of the event, and who they want to talk to.

4. Given that we're generally networking in the context of developing our business, it stands to reason that a lot of the conversation will be business-based. However, in a one-to-one, you have the extra time to find out about the person behind the business. As we've just seen in my story about Steve, it is often the 'stuff' about them that makes it possible to build a rapport strong enough to pass them really good referrals.

5. One-to-one meetings can be held anywhere; a typical venue would be the local coffee shop, as it is on 'neutral' ground and will likely be convenient for both parties. However, there is another option. Why not try holding the meeting at one of the respective partners' place of business?

    There is a significant benefit to doing this, particularly for the partner that is on 'away' ground. When you visit someone's place of business, you get to learn so much about their business. What is their team like? What's up on the walls? Even if you know the person well, you'll learn entirely new things about their business.

6. To finish, one for us Unnatural Networkers. When we discussed exiting a comfortable conversation in Chapter 6, it was like we were forcing ourselves back into the abyss. In a one-to-one meeting, that feeling doesn't exist! You're only ever going to be talking to one person, and the introvert in you will be excellent at finding out the interesting connections between the two of you.

Listening is better than talking!

You should be able to see then that one-to-ones are the best way to build relationships. So before we start to look in detail at how to conduct a one-to-one, it would be useful to consider how we can maximise the chance of building relationships effectively in a one-to-one meeting.

It all comes down to one thing: it is better to be listening than talking. The vast majority of people like nothing more than to talk about themselves. This means that if we are listening intently, and taking in what we're being told, then our partner is going to think we're brilliant.

This will make it more likely that they will then try to help us out. Obviously, if both parties have read this book and are only going to try to listen, then it won't be much of a meeting! However, as a general rule, try to make more of the meeting about the other person.

To do this, we need to be good listeners – so here are a few tips on how to listen effectively:

1. **Get rid of all distractions**: that means turning off your mobile and laptop. Nothing shows more disrespect than interrupting someone's flow because a message or call has come in. Equally, if meeting in your own premises, make sure none of your team members come in to disturb you.

2. **Give adequate time**: if you have to rush through a one-to-one, it is inevitable that the conversation won't be of such high quality. How long should a one-to-one take? The answer to that is 'however long it takes', but if you allow an hour, that's a good starting point.

3. **Make sure you concentrate**: to be a good listener, you need to make sure that you are listening properly to everything the other person says.

When your partner is talking, it is very easy to spend the time thinking about and formulating your next response. I know I've done it! But if you're doing that, you can't be 100% focused on what's being said.

4. **Take notes**: making notes about what your partner is saying is a very powerful way of showing that you are listening. You wouldn't be able to write anything down if you weren't listening, would you? Taking notes will make your partner feel as though what they're saying is important.

5. **Show that you are listening by asking suitable questions**: from time to time it may be appropriate to seek clarification on what your partner means. When you ask your question, if you repeat the wording/phrasing that they used, it is a very clear sign that you've been listening well.

6. **Don't interrupt!** Fairly obvious, this one! If you are only interested in getting your point of view across, you're not going to be doing much listening.

7. **Ask open-ended questions**: this is an interesting one, because most of the items on this list are things that you react to, whereas here you can be more proactive. Asking questions like 'How do you feel about X?' can't generally be answered in one word. The response has to go into more detail, which gives you, the listener, more chance to listen.

8. **Mirror body language**: this is a very simple trick that helps build rapport when in a conversation. Feed off your partner's body language: if they lean in, do the same. If they maintain eye contact at a particular moment, do the same. If they smile, smile back.

9. **Their issues are important**: there will, of course, be occasions when you don't agree with your partner, or perhaps you just don't believe that something important to them is relevant. But the key is in those words: if it is important to them, it is important. You underestimate that at your peril in relationship-building terms.

10. **'You have two ears and one mouth'** as the old expression goes and it is best to use them proportionally.

Not all one-to-one meetings are the same

It is very tempting to think that all one-to-one meetings should follow the same sort of format. As an Unnatural Networker, wouldn't it be easier if there was just a set agenda to follow? Unfortunately, it doesn't quite work out like that. The agenda for your one-to-one will be governed by the level and quality of the relationship that already exists between the two partners.

Here are two questions that you may want to ask at a one-to-one:

- What do you do?

- Could you get me an introduction to your best client?

Would it be appropriate to ask the first question of someone you've known well for 10 years? I think not. Why on earth would you be asking someone you know really well what they do?

Equally, imagine you're sitting down for the very first time with someone you've just met. Could you realistically get away with asking them the second question? No! Until we've got the right level of credibility with the other person, there's no way we should be asking for an introduction to their best client!

So, the type of one-to-one you have comes down to how good the relationship is between the two people. I categorise one-to-ones into three types.

Initially, we start off with a basic relationship-building one-to-one, where we find out about the person. Secondly, we move on to a business-building one-to-one. Here, the basics we need to know about our partner are in place. It's just a question of getting specific about how we can help them.

Lastly comes the 'let's just get on with it' one-to-one (catchy title, I know). Here, there's no need to find out any of the basics. We just want to know how we can help each other as quickly as possible given that we're both busy people.

Basic relationship-building one-to-one

This level of one-to-one meeting is exactly what it sounds like: a chance to start building a relationship with someone. This form of one-to-one is particularly important in a networking group environment. There's only so much you can learn from listening to someone present their business for 60 seconds. To get to know someone properly, you need to sit down with them at a one-to-one.

These are the sorts of questions to ask:

- What do you do?

- Where are you based?

- Where do you cover geographically?

- What are your goals for your business?

- When did you start doing what you do?

- Why do you do what you do?

- What are your accomplishments in business?

- How did you get into what you do?

- What are the latest trends in your industry?

- What excites you about what you do?

- What networks are you in?

- What specific skills do you bring to your business?

- Who is a good contact for you to meet?

- Why would you be interested in making contacts with *accountants*?

- How do you help your clients?

- What are your interests?

Now, you may have noticed that some of these questions are familiar. Well, they are. Many are the same questions you'd ask in a conversation at a networking event.

Of course, if you already know the answers from when you met them the first time, you've done some of the basics. In which case, you're ready to move on to the next type of one-to-one.

Business-building one-to-one

So, we've covered the basics. We have a relationship with our partner. We know about their business, we know that we are both good at what we do. We now need to improve the chance of being able to refer business to each other.

Here is a table with some suggested questions for a business-building one-to-one. You'll see the questions in the left-hand column, and then some insight into WHY it is a good idea to ask each of the questions on the right-hand side:

Question	Why?
Who are your top three current clients?	• Knowing who the person's current clients are could mean potential referral opportunities for you. • If you know your partner's current clients, you can match up referral possibilities from your own network in similar industries. For example, if they do a lot of work with accountants, you could introduce them to more accountants. • It is important to know what level someone is working at. There's a big difference, for example, between building a website for a local corner store and building a website for Tesco.
Why do your clients think you are good?	• This is the ultimate question to help build credibility. It's all well and good hearing your partner tell you why they're good, but if it comes from their clients, that's even stronger. • It becomes much easier to recommend your partner with this knowledge. • The best answers to this question will come in the form of a story – we'll find out why stories are more engaging in Chapter 8.

Who are your top three target clients?	• To know who your partner wants referrals to – you may be able to help! • If you don't share who your top three (or five, or ten) target clients are, how will anyone else possibly know?! We'll look more at target clients in Chapter 9.
What's the best way to introduce you to a target client?	• Even if your partner can help you with your specific referral request, they won't be able to unless they know what to say to them. • Whatever we say needs to get over the initial barrier 'but I already have a good accountant'. Client success stories are the best way to do this.
Who typically passes business to you as an introducer?	• Introducers are brilliant for business. Instead of receiving a referral to a single end user, you could receive a referral to someone who'll pass you 10/100/1000 end users. • The question also gets people thinking about where their business comes from, and may help them if they are struggling with specific referral targets.
How did your best referral happen?	• Hearing how referrals occurred is usually fascinating. It will likely involve some sort of story, which will be interesting. • There is the chance for the situation to be replicated.

What can I watch/listen out for to get you a referral?	• This is an alternative approach to find business for someone. It involves training people to look or listen out for given situations. For example, someone complaining about their computer being slow = opportunity for IT professional.
	• By 'planting seeds' in the minds of our networking contacts, we can get them looking for business opportunities for us when we're not even there.

These questions are primarily intended for our one-to-one partner. However, one-to-ones should help us to grow our own business too. So if these questions are important, how can we make sure our partner asks us these questions?

It's very simple! All you have to do is take these questions along to the one-to-one, and ask your partner to ask you them!

'Let's just get on with it' one-to-one

When we know the person and their business well, there is clearly no need to go into some of the basic relationship-building details. What we really want to do at this stage is help each other grow our businesses.

There is only one real difference between this advanced one-to-one and the business-building one-to-one we've just looked at. The questions you'd ask of your partner are very similar.

The key difference is that instead of just listening and taking down notes on what your partner is saying, the whole meeting is focused around making introductions that will help each party move their business forward. So the meeting would be run asking questions like:

- Who are you looking to speak to in business at the moment?

- These are the people I've been dealing with recently – who would you like an introduction to?

Having asked these questions, it's then about action. So instead of writing down a list of follow up actions, you just get on with it and pick up the phone to the appropriate people.

Case Study: Let's just get on with it

I was chatting with the noted networking expert Phil Berg recently, and he was telling me how he generates referrals in a one-to-one meeting. There are two key ingredients. Firstly, he makes sure that he only focuses on his partner's business in the one-to-one. He calls this the 'away leg': if he only focuses on the other person, then he knows there will be a 'home leg' coming soon.

Secondly, he explains how important it is to have the necessary time. For this meeting, he says, you need two hours. Occasionally people ask him why they need to spend so long. Phil's answer to them is fascinating: he tells them to stop looking at it like a one-to-one meeting. Instead, take the mindset that it is a business meeting, with a business person, focused on generating business.

Then, it's a three-stage process to generate referrals:

1. He spends the first 20 minutes extracting a list of about 10 target contacts. The more you have on the list, the more chance of getting a referral.

2. Phil then spends the next 40 minutes role-playing the 'angle of attack'. The key here is to get the person to say 'Yes, I'll take a call from X'. To get a yes, the angle of attack has to be more than simply 'I know a good printer, would you like to speak to them?' The chances are most people won't say yes to that question. There has to be a solid reason WHY they would want to talk to them (and we'll look into these reasons more in Chapter 9).

3. Lastly, Phil picks up the phone and calls his contacts. This involves a small white lie in that he will never say he is sitting with his one-to-one partner while calling, as this would put too much pressure on the person being called. But he says something like: 'I was chatting to a mate, Charlie, yesterday. Charlie has helped me out recently, so I asked him how I could help him. Charlie said he'd love introductions to good people in the printing industry – and I immediately thought of you. I'd like to get Charlie to call you, I really think it would be worth the two of you speaking.'

Let's be clear here. This technique of generating business in the middle of the meeting is an advanced networking technique. As an Unnatural Networker, I can appreciate the discomfort in this approach: however, the rewards can be fantastic.

My advice would be to stick to what you're comfortable with, and build up gradually to this sort of one-to-one meeting.

The most important questions of all

Hopefully, by reading this chapter you'll have a strong feeling for how important one-to-one meetings are in networking. But we haven't yet discussed the two most important questions to ask at a one-to-one. It is vital that they should be included in every single one-to-one that we ever have:

- What follow up actions do we both have?

This question is vital. It is about where networking really starts to work: the follow up. This topic is so important, it takes a whole chapter to cover it. We'll look at follow up in Chapter 11.

- When's our next one-to-one?

This question is equally important. There's a common misconception that once you've had a one-to-one with someone, you're done. There's no need to go back to them because you know everything there is to know about them.

That is wrong, on a number of levels:

- You can't possibly get to know everything about someone in a one-hour meeting.

- Over time, you can very easily forget what you've discussed.

- Things change: especially in business, we don't always work with the same clients, or have the same goals.

Crucially though, one-to-ones are about relationship-building. That means we are on a journey, not heading for a single destination. So agree then and there, in your one-to-one, when your next meeting will be.

Chapter 7 Action Points

- Book a one-to-one with a big fish new contact that you meet at a networking event. Note the difference between this one-to-one…

- … and the one-to-one that you set up with an existing contact with whom you already have a good relationship.

- Prepare your list of questions that you're going to ask at your one-to-one.

- Print out two copies, and give one copy to your one-to-one partner to ask you.

- Agree your follow up actions, and book your next one-to-one.

PART 3

Presenting your Business

Time for a recap.

If you've been keeping up so far, we, the Unnatural Networkers of this world, have actually gone networking. That's right: we've realised that networking is worthwhile, and worked out where we should network.

Then we got ourselves prepared, found some people to talk to, and not only that, kept them engaged in interesting conversation! At the same time, we managed to avoid people who didn't want to talk to us, and even got out of conversations that were dull and uninteresting. Finally, we also carried on the conversation with a big fish over a cup of coffee in a one-to-one.

It's now time to get ready for a different type of networking. Many networks offer the chance for attendees to give a short presentation about their business.

Strong contact networking groups operate under this structure: the meeting starts with an open networking free-for-all, but then is run to a tight timetable. Members get 60 seconds to present their business or service, followed by one member getting 10 minutes to go into more detail, perhaps showing some slides or a product demonstration.

Other networks will have slightly different arrangements, but at virtually every one, you, the attendee, will get the chance to present your business.

This leads us Unnatural Networkers to a challenge! We've got to be ready to talk about our business in a confident and professional way. Not only that, we've got to encourage other people to want to help us to find business. That's right: we're moving out of our comfort zone again!

We've now got to stand up in front of a roomful of people and speak. Public speaking is something that many people find difficult, and not just Unnatural Networkers. It is said that public speaking is one of the human race's greatest fears, coming above the fear of death. (For more information on this, read Andy Lopata and Peter Roper's excellent book '...And Death Came Third!')

I'm going to divide this topic into three chapters. Firstly, in Chapter 8, we'll look at what you're going to say in your presentation. Next, in Chapter 9, we'll look at the concept of target market. This is where we try to focus our presentation on ensuring we get the referrals that we want. Finally, in Chapter 10, we'll put the presentation together, and think about actually delivering it.

CHAPTER 8

Storytelling

What am I going to say?

This is the first thing to consider when presenting. There is absolutely no point in getting psyched up to speak to a roomful of people, then wondering what you're actually going to say. So, start with preparing WHAT you're going to say.

To help figure this out, think about what the goal of the presentation is. This is what we know:

- We need to get over as clearly as we can what we actually do, and how we add value to our customers. All in only 60 seconds!

- We're networking, so the primary goal has to be to build relationships, not to hard sell.

- Being given time to present is a golden opportunity to demonstrate our credibility. Ideally we want the people who hear our presentation to be able and ready to find us some business. Can we demonstrate our credibility enough to be referred on?

- As Unnatural Networkers, we're out of our comfort zone already. We therefore really want people to listen to our presentation and be genuinely interested. There's nothing worse than feeling like you're boring everyone to tears...

Let me tell you a story

I think, perhaps, that telling a story might be the best way to illustrate what I'm trying to say, so here we go:

The story is about Deena, who is a lettings agent in Doncaster, south Yorkshire. Deena is a BNI member, and I heard this story at a training event I was hosting recently.

Deena received a call in her office at about 5.00pm on a February afternoon. On this particular day, it was raining. Being February, it was also virtually dark.

The person on the line was a lady, and it was clear very quickly to Deena that she was upset and in a bit of a state. It transpired that she had just been kicked out of the house where she lived by her now ex-partner. And it wasn't just her: with her were her two kids, both under the age of five. Essentially, she was standing there on the pavement outside the house, with a couple of suitcases, three boxes, and two very young children. Indeed, what a nice guy.

The lady, speaking as best she could through her tears, was asking Deena, as a lettings agent, whether she had any properties to let. And obviously, given it was a dark, cold, rainy night in February, was there anything available right now?

Now, I don't know a huge amount about the world of property lettings. However, I do know that you can't just click your fingers and a flat or house will magically appear. There is due process to go through: contracts, payments, reference checking, inventories and plenty more besides, not least of which is whether there is actually a vacant property somewhere.

Clearly, none of this due process could realistically be followed when Deena received that phone call. But she said that she'd see what she could do to help. Fortunately, a flat was available nearby, so she told the lady that she'd happily let her and her kids take the flat for the night. Then, in the morning, they could sit down and sort out the necessary paperwork and payment.

Deena was then just about to finish the conversation when she remembered that the lady was standing outside her old house with her children and all of her possessions. Without even thinking about it, Deena asked her if she would like picking up. Her offer was gratefully accepted, so she drove over to pick them up, took them to the new flat and made sure they were settled.

So – end of story.

I have a question for you. Would you, assuming you were in a position to do so, be prepared to refer business to Deena? I'm virtually 100% sure anyone's response would be yes.

I now want to ask another question: why? Why would you be prepared to refer business to Deena?

My guess is your answer could be any one (or more) of the following:

- Great customer service

- Went the extra mile

- Sorted out a problem

- Got a good result

- Cared about the customer

- Didn't worry about the money

All of those would doubtless be fair responses. However, I think there is another reason why you would be prepared to refer business to Deena.

It's very simple: I told you a story.

Many people spend their time networking telling people what they do. Sometimes people talk about how they do what they do.

But really good networkers ignore both the 'what' and the 'how' because they are too focused on the other party. It is much better to look at how we help our clients, and how they feel about our service.

How do you think the lady in the story feels about Deena?

What you'll often hear...

Compare Deena's story to the following, a typical presentation you will hear when networking:

'Good morning, I'm Charlie Lawson, from ABC Lettings Ltd. ABC Lettings Ltd offers a full range of property-related services to businesses across the whole of north-west London. We've been in business since 1954, and are based on the high street, just past Maxwell Road.

We can help you with all sorts of property letting and management related issues: we can market your property, manage your property, and deal with tenants so that you don't have to. We can help you with inventories, we can sort out contracts, and we can collect the rent on your behalf.

ABC Lettings Ltd covers properties in the Rickmansworth, Watford, Northwood, Ruislip, Pinner and Eastcote areas. ABC Lettings Ltd works closely with brand new property investors, landlords with two or three properties, and bigger landlords with a large portfolio of properties. Through our many years of experience, we are able to offer unrivalled service and customer support to all of our clients to cover any of their property and property management needs.

Thank you for listening, I'm Charlie Lawson from ABC Lettings Ltd.'

Let's ask the same question on refer-ability that we asked ourselves after Deena's story. Assuming you were in a position to do so, would you refer business to Charlie Lawson of ABC Lettings Ltd? Would the answer be so positive? Despite hearing about literally everything ABC Lettings does, would anyone really be in a position to confidently refer business to them?

The presentation also made a point of talking about how good their customer service is. Do we believe this? Would the lettings agent (or indeed anyone in business) ever actually say they DON'T offer good customer service?

Telling your listeners that you offer good customer service isn't enough; proof is required. Deena's story doesn't mention customer service once, and yet her commitment to it is stamped all over it.

Hopefully, the message you'll have picked up from this is to **tell stories**! Let's look at some of the reasons why stories make so much sense.

Stories are more interesting

Stories are more interesting than a bunch of facts. There's an old saying: 'Facts tell, stories sell', and it is true. When we hear stories, we immediately put ourselves in the shoes of the protagonists. We want to know what happens. We want to know that there is a happy ending.

Instead of focusing on being transactional, stories make us more relational. We've already seen that being relational should be our aim when networking.

One of our goals when presenting our business was to make sure that our audience is genuinely interested in what we are saying. As the presenter, boring them to tears would make us feel terrible. Stories will mean that your audience will listen to you and engage more in what you are saying.

Have a look around the room as you tell a story. Every single pair of eyes will be focused on you. Look around the room while someone is presenting their business like the other lettings agent, and you'll see a very different picture.

As long as you stick to these key rules on storytelling, your presentations will instantly become more powerful and impactful.

Challenge	Solution
It's not about you	Focus the story on your customer and how you helped them.
What you ACTUALLY DO is often quite boring...	... in terms of the story. Remember Deena? We didn't hear or need the minutiae about how she sorted out the rental flat.
There is no one to root for	All good stories have heroes. Make sure your story has a hero too (clue – that's you!)
There isn't an issue	For the hero to do their work, there must be a villain too. Clearly we're not talking about an actual villain (I'm picturing a James Bond baddie, stroking his white cat whilst plotting to take over the world...)

There has to be a situation that the customer is facing: perhaps they needed to save money, they were inefficient, they were frustrated about some aspect of their business. |
| The story is lacking in emotion | Talk about how the customer felt before you provided your service and what they thought about you afterwards. |

Making Stories Human

I was discussing storytelling at a training session, and a lady who ran a payroll company was having some challenges getting her head around the emotional/human side of her services. Exasperated, she said: "Look, I get how some professions are just more interesting, but come on, I do payroll. What's interesting and emotional about that?"

I asked her about the last client she'd worked with. She told me how she'd helped an entrepreneur set up a payroll scheme, saving him approximately £2,000 a year against the current scheme he was using. In addition though, his old scheme was now unlawful. Her 'uninteresting' and 'unemotional' payroll services were now saving someone £2,000 a year, and potentially keeping him out of jail!

It's just about finding the human angle to the story.

Stories help you break down your business

60 seconds isn't long. Given that many networking events will only give you 60 seconds to speak, how on earth do you cover your entire business in that time? Even with five or ten minutes, it isn't easy. So don't try to do it! If you try and tell people about everything you do, at best you will only ever end up just listing all of your products or services, like our lettings agent friend above.

This reminds me of seeing a florist present her business recently, and she started by saying: "Hi, my name is Laura, and I'm a florist. Everyone knows what a florist does, so I won't bore you with that…"

To be honest, I don't remember what else she said in her presentation. All I could think about was that I know a florist deals with flowers: but I don't know anything like enough about what a florist does to find her any business.

So I made a point of having a chat with Laura after the meeting, and told her that I didn't really know what a florist does. She answered that she dealt in all areas of floristry, to which I replied: "OK, what does that mean?"

So I asked her some questions. Did she do a delivery service? Did she do weddings? Did she do funerals? Did she do corporate flowers? Was she part of the Interflora network?

The answer to all these questions was yes, but it wasn't until I'd asked these questions that I had a true idea of what she did. More importantly, I could now think about finding business for her.

When you're networking, keep it simple, and break down your business into its constituent parts. When you're given an opportunity to present your business, just pick one of those parts.

So, instead of trying to generalise every aspect of her business, Laura could have said 'Today, I'm going to talk about our floral wedding service…' Then she could tell a story about how she'd helped a client who was getting married, and how happy they were with her service.

Stories mean you don't sell to the room

We know by now that networking is about building relationships. If we go networking trying to sell, we'll be doomed to failure, because no one ever goes networking with the intention of buying anything.

Now, let's transfer this idea to presenting your business. Remember, if no one there is going to buy your product, it is pointless selling your services to the room. Here are two good reasons why:

1. In networking groups, there is an understanding that the members are there to help each other with growing their business by passing referrals. Indeed, in strong contact networking groups, there is an expectation that the members will bring referrals.

It is a complete waste of time selling to the room, because if anyone needs your product or service, they're likely to use you anyway!

2. Selling to the room is not only a complete waste of time, it is a wasted opportunity. We saw in Chapter 2 that everyone you are presenting your business to will have, on average, 1,000 contacts.

So, if the meeting you're at has 40 people there, the potential demand for your product or service isn't just the 40 people in the room. Instead, those 40 people are your potential salesforce who could get you access to up to 40,000 people.

So your presentation on your business is aimed at helping you get referrals to the contacts of the people who hear it. Telling a story will maximise the chance of that happening.

The worst case of selling to the room I've ever seen...

In his presentation, an independent financial advisor announced that he was going to talk about his critical illness policy, and how important it was to be well covered. He then went around the room, pointing to different people, saying: "You've got my policy so you'll be fine; you haven't though, so you're in trouble – you have, you haven't", and so on.

Was this a good presentation on his business? No! Firstly, he was clearly breaking client confidentialities. Secondly, and crucially, he was limiting potential demand for his product to just the people in the room.

Chapter 8 Action Points

- Break down the constituent parts of your business, and choose one to focus your presentation on.

- Within that part of your business, think of a story about how you helped a client. Remember, the focus must be on what the client thought about you, not what you did for the client.

- Practise delivering your story. Aim for about 30-40 seconds.

CHAPTER 9

Target Market

Telling stories is a good start. However, to generate referrals from our networking contacts, we have to do more. Stories alone won't be enough to generate business.

The next step when preparing your presentation on your business is to think about what you want. In Chapter 3, we discussed referrals: getting opportunities to present yourself to someone in the market for your product or service.

We come now to discussing a truism of networking: the more you focus on the target market that you want, the more referral business you'll get. You may think that you're cutting yourself out of opportunities by focusing in, but it just doesn't work like that.

The more specific you are, the more business will come your way.

Anybody + Everybody + Somebody = Nobody!

Here's the challenge. If you include the words 'anybody', 'everybody', or 'somebody', then your result in terms of referrals will be 'nobody'. Let me try to illustrate this.

I was at a BNI meeting recently, and an osteopath stood up to deliver his presentation. He finished by saying: "A good referral for me would be anybody with a back." How many people do you know that have a back?!

Did the osteopath get any business? No. Not a single opportunity. The secret here is that we have to be more specific about what we're after. As it turns out, the more specific, the better. This story illustrates this very nicely:

I was running a business generation exercise a few years ago, where all the attendees (about 60) were asked to share their top 'target' in terms of who they'd like a referral to.

The key to success in this exercise is that it only works if the targets shared are specific. That means that we need to name a target company, but on top of that, we also really need the name and job title of the person at the company they'd need to speak to.

We'd just started the exercise when I was confronted by a lady who ran an events company. I could tell from her body language and the look on her face that she thought the whole process was a joke.

However, loving a challenge, I asked her who her dream referral request was. While her body language and facial expressions were bad, they were nothing compared to her reaction when she spoke to me. "It is absolutely inconceivable that anyone in this room will know the person I need to speak to," was her answer.

"Go on, just give it a go," I replied.

"Seriously, it won't work, just move on to the next person," she replied, folding her arms, and by now sounding a little cross.

"Just give it a try. You never know," I ventured.

"Look, I've told you already," she answered, "all the people in this room run small businesses. It is absolutely inconceivable that anyone will know the marketing director of the Hilton Hotel Group, so it's not even worth wasting my time."

Before I could respond, the gentleman just two seats away from her said: "I don't know the marketing director of Hilton Hotels, but my next door neighbour is the group chairman. Would that be of any use to you?"

"Er, yes – I guess it would…"

It's incredible. When out networking, we so often close our minds to the opportunities that are sitting (literally) right next to us. It isn't about the people in the room. It's about who those people know, and whether our relationship with them is good enough to allow us to get an introduction.

When we ask for referrals, we're obviously talking about business, and typically, we'll be talking to business people. Of course, plenty of referral opportunities come through specific requests to clients or suppliers (i.e. contacts from a business point of view), but so many more come from examples like the story above.

In that case, it was a next door neighbour. But it could be a contact at the gym, or someone who sends their kids to the same school as your children, or an old school friend.

Being specific requires you to be able to name your referral requests in terms of:

- The target company

- The target person in terms of their job title, and best of all...

- The target person's name

I appreciate that in the Hilton Hotels story above, we didn't hear a target name. It won't always be necessary. However, wherever possible it is worth including the name. Personal relationships are so often the key to making referral connections happen.

But I just don't know how...

So, we've had a look at WHY being specific is important. There's another angle we need to cover. Let me tell you about Julia, who runs a Virtual PA business. She asked me the same question that I've heard countless times before from other networkers: "I know I should be specific, but HOW do I actually do it?"

Well, all you need is a money funnel. It goes like this:

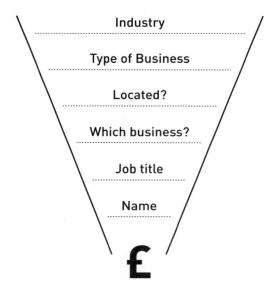

The key is getting started with the funnel. The first step is to identify the industry you want to work with, and this is often where business owners get stuck!

Julia offers her Virtual PA service to businesses, which makes her a Business-to-Business (B2B) operator. The question I asked was a simple one:

"Who's your best current client?"

This is a good place to start, for a couple of reasons. Firstly, if we're not sure who to ask for, we might as well go for similar businesses that are likely to be good clients too. (I accept that it may not always be appropriate to work for a direct competitor of a current client.)

Secondly, when it comes to speaking to the target business, it is really important to be able to provide some evidence of how you've helped a similar company.

Julia's answer to this was a chiropractor, so immediately that brings us to the health and wellness industry. I then just asked her the following questions, filling in the funnel as we went:

- "Would another chiropractor be good, or is there any other profession (within health and wellness) that would be good for you?"

She told me that a doctors' surgery would be a good opportunity for her.

- "Where would you like this doctors' surgery to be located?"

South-east London.

- "Which doctors' surgery in south-east London?"

The Hurley Clinic in Kennington.

- "Who would you need to speak to at the Hurley Clinic in Kennington?"

The practice manager.

- "Do you know the name of the practice manager at the Hurley Clinic in Kennington?"

I've no idea.

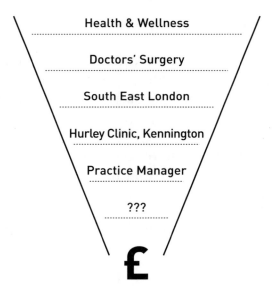

There will often be a point when you don't know the answer to one of the questions, like Julia found with the last one. However, it isn't difficult to get the information we need. All it needs is some research: Google or LinkedIn will get you the answer 99% of the time.

In Julia's case, it didn't take long to find out that the practice manager was Steven Hunt.

And with that, Julia had successfully managed to be specific. A good referral for her is Steven Hunt, the practice manager of the Hurley Clinic in Kennington, south-east London.

Julia's block with this, in common with many other networkers, was just getting started.

Stuck with your specific?

The simplest way to do this is to think of your best current client, and decide whether you'd like another client like them. Then, name the industry they're in. Once within that industry, think of the type of business you would like to speak to. Then, pick a business and work out which job title you need to speak to. Lastly, do some research on LinkedIn to get you the name of the person.

But I want to talk to individuals!

Now, you may be thinking that this is all well and good, but Julia is a Business-to-Business operator. What about me? I don't sell my service to other businesses. My customer base is the population at large. As a Business-to-Consumer (B2C) operator, who can I possibly ask for specifically?

Remember, the same rules apply: if we ask for anybody / everybody / somebody, we'll end up with nobody. It would also be too specific to say 'I'd like a referral to Mrs Baker, who lives at 22 Murray Road...' That just isn't practical. It would also cause client confidentiality issues for many businesses.

A good example would be our osteopath friend from earlier, who, if you remember, asked for anyone with a back. After I heard that presentation, I went and had a chat with him. His name was Roger, and he said to me that he understood how being specific is possible when asking for business: you just pick a business. "But what about me?" he said. "Literally anyone is a potential customer for me. Everyone has a back!"

The problem with that is it doesn't help his networking contacts to help him.

But there is a better way. In much the same way as before, I just asked Roger about his best current client. He told me that he'd done a lot of work with a rugby player, who'd suffered a string of niggling back injuries.

I then put two questions to Roger:

1. "Would you like more clients like this one?"

Response: "Of course."

2. "So, where do people like this 'hang out'?" By hang out, I'm not talking about which pub they go to; what we mean by this is 'where can you get

access to people like this?' Could Roger set up a situation where someone refers him to a stream of rugby players?

In Roger's case, it's not too hard to work out where to find more rugby players. All we then had to do was fill up his funnel.

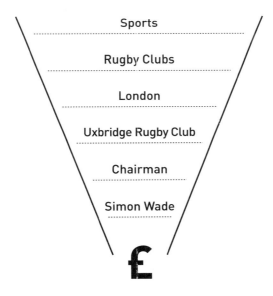

By asking the same questions we went through with Julia, he successfully filled up his funnel. A good referral for him, then, was Simon Wade, the chairman of Uxbridge Rugby Club. Easy!

So, the technique here is again to think about a good current client. What sort of person are they? Then think *where do they 'hang out'*?

It may be they can be found in a certain place, as Roger found, or perhaps you'll need to build relationships with a particular person who knows the sort of people you'd like to do business with. For example, if you want to talk to people who live in a big house: who might know those people? A financial advisor maybe, or an estate agent?

Once you've worked out where your target market 'hangs out', treat the introducer as the referral request, not the end user. The great point about this technique is that it then becomes just like a Business-to-Business specific referral request. You just have to name the company, the job title and the name.

But whether you are B2B or B2C, the same simple starting point applies. For us Unnatural Networkers, that's really important because we need things to be simple to make sure we do them.

All you need to be specific is to think about a good current client, and then think *where do I get another one of those?*

Why would my target want to talk to me?

Now, as an Unnatural Networker, this is an obvious question. When you present your business, you can tell the best story, and be absolutely specific in what you're asking for – but there's still a crucial part missing.

Why would my specific referral request want to talk to me?

At another business generation session, like the one where the lady got a potential introduction to Hilton Hotels, an attendee stood up. It became clear that he also didn't really buy into the process, but for a different reason.

"If it's so easy to just name the person that would be my dream referral – then fine: I'd like a referral to Sir Richard Branson please."

He then sat down, arms folded, looking pleased with himself. I then asked him a question: "OK, that's fine, but why would Sir Richard Branson want to talk to you?"

At this, he had no response. When networking, whenever we ask for a specific referral request, it is absolutely vital to get across clearly why your referral target would want to speak to you.

By the way, the answer to that question can't be: 'because I want to sell my product/service to them'. We've got to come up with something much more compelling than that.

So, what can we say to back up our referral requests? The answer is very simple: it comes in the stories that we tell about how we've helped a client.

Telling a story about how you helped a similar client to your target will provide ample evidence that it would be worth making the introduction for you. Did you save that client money? Did you make that client more efficient? Did you make that client more profitable? Did you allow that client to spend more time with their family?

In a referral, there are three parties: you – the service provider; the client – who buys the product or service; and the introducer – who knows you and the client. When asking for referrals, the only person that matters is the introducer. You not only need to make them confident that you'd do a great job, but more importantly, you need to show them how THEIR credibility will increase by making the introduction.

So, for example, if you're after a referral to an accountancy practice, preface that referral request by telling a story about how you've helped A.N. Other Accountants provide a better service to their clients. Or, if you're after a referral to a web designer, first tell a story about how you helped an existing web designer become more profitable.

Then, when it comes to your contact making the introduction to your dream referral, they can refer you with confidence because they know that making that introduction is going to make them look good.

Chapter 9 Action Points

- Work out who your dream referral would be by filling out your own funnel. Start by thinking of a good current client.

- That will give you the industry, then pick a company. Sometimes you'll need to research suitable companies on Google/LinkedIn.

- Think about the job level you'd need to speak to, and then research to find the person's name.

- Consider asking for introducers, rather than end users. Then follow the same process as above to pick out a specific name.

- Repeat the process to come up with a top 10 list of target clients. Print your list and carry it with you.

- Share your target list with people you've got a good relationship with.

- Work out the compelling reason for why your target client would want to speak to you.

CHAPTER 10

Delivering your Presentation

Putting the presentation together

Let's put Chapters 7 and 8 together, and create our full presentation. We'll assume for the purposes of this exercise that the presentation is 60 seconds in length.

Introduction

This should be no longer than 10 seconds as an absolute maximum! The content for this section should be the same every single time you present, and is really aimed at anyone in the room who doesn't know you. All you need to do is get across your name and what you do, so everyone in the room knows what you do. For example:

> *"Good morning, I'm Charlie Lawson from*
> *ABC Web Designers Ltd."*

Depending on your profession, you may need to use a few more words here. However, as long as the audience are clear on what you do, that's all you need. Clearly, for anyone that already knows you and your business this is largely irrelevant, but the interesting section is just coming up.

Tell a Story

So, a couple of quick reminders: break down your business into its constituent parts, and share a quick story about how you helped a client. Remember to make it clear how the client felt before they came to you, and how they felt about you afterwards.

> "I'd like to tell you about Steve – a new client that I took on recently. Steve runs an Accountancy practice and he came to me very worried, because he was really struggling to bring in new business, and was facing having to lay off a key member of his team. His website was generating him absolutely nothing at all, and was costing him maintenance charges of £200 per month.
>
> I was able to set him up with a new website which is completely updateable by his team at the touch of a button. Within the first month of its launch, his company is on the first page of Google, and has received as many enquiries as he did in the previous 12 months through his old website.
>
> Not only that, he was telling me that the website has already easily paid for itself, and there's no need to lay off any staff. He is so happy that he has also referred me two contacts of his that are interested in updating their online presence."

The Ask

Remember: we need to be specific in who we're asking for, right down to the name of the person!

> "A good referral for me this week would be to speak to other accountancy practices –
>
> in particular, Joe Bloggs, lead partner of XYZ Accountants Ltd based in Rickmansworth."

Justify the Ask

Your networking contacts are going to need to know what they should say if they know your specific referral request. Remember, we can't just say 'because I want to sell them my product...'

> *"I'd like to speak to Joe because his company's website is very similar to my clients' old website. I'd like to help him see similar returns through his web presence."*

Sign Off

It is essential to say your name at the end of your presentation, although you might ask why this is necessary given that you announced it at the start. The simple answer to this is people weren't listening properly at the start. Either they weren't paying attention, or just didn't pick up your name.

However, if your story piqued their interest, or perhaps they know your specific referral request or know someone who does, it makes sense to reaffirm your name so they can make a note to talk to you afterwards. It also finishes off your presentation nicely.

> *"Thank you for listening, I'm Charlie Lawson from ABC Web Designers Ltd."*

Now it's your turn!

Use this template to write a 60-second presentation for your business:

Introduction

....

....

....

Tell a Story

....

....

....

....

....

....

....

....

....

The Ask

....

....

....

....

....

Justify the Ask

....

....

....

....

....

....

Sign Off

....

....

....

Presentation mastery

You now have the basis of a presentation, but that isn't the end of it. Some more work is required! This will depend on the type of networking event you go to. At a strong contact networking group, you'll deliver a 60-second presentation every meeting.

How do you think it would go down if you told the same story every time you spoke? Clearly, that would get boring very quickly, so we need to develop lots of different stories to illustrate what our clients think of us.

Each client, each bit of work you do for a client, even an individual conversation with a client, could provide you with the basis of a story. You don't need to cover your entire history with a particular client in one story. This does take time to prepare: but as the saying goes, the secret to success without hard work is still a secret.

If your networking is less structured, and you're attending open networking events, then getting one presentation really polished and practised is OK, because different audiences will hear it each time.

It is also worth considering that the content of the presentation should form the basis of individual conversations (as covered in Chapter 6). Remember, we are just as interested in keeping people's attention in a conversation as in a presentation.

Not every presentation is 60 seconds long!

We've looked in detail at a 60-second presentation, but not every networking event will offer this timeframe. Whether you're given two minutes, five minutes or ten minutes, keep the rough structure the same. In other words, spend the majority of the time telling stories, then focus on specific referral requests and justifying who you're asking for. Your introduction and sign off should still be only the minor parts of the presentation.

Delivering the best possible presentation

Some years ago, I had a conversation with a BNI member after a meeting. I asked him how BNI was working for him, and it was clear from our discussion that he was an Unnatural Networker just like me. He consistently had to push himself to go networking, but he really enjoyed it when he did go. In fact he said he was starting to find it very rewarding, so I asked him what sort of business he was getting from his group. His response fascinated me.

"Oh, I'm happy with the business I'm getting, but that's not the reason why I find it so rewarding."

He then went on to tell me that his daughter had just got married. Ever since she'd been born, some 30 years previously, he'd been dreading the fact that one day he would have to deliver a father-of-the-bride speech.

But then, all of a sudden, he realised he'd done the speech and not really thought about it. He was questioning himself why this might have been: and then it hit him. It was the fact that he'd been attending his BNI meeting once a week, and delivering his 60-second presentation to his fellow members. He'd been practising for his daughter's wedding speech without even realising it!

When it came to the big day, he was subconsciously treating the guests as though they were his networking contacts.

Becoming good at presentations is all about practice, and that heads my list of ten presentation tips to help you deliver the best possible presentation every time.

1. **Practise, practise, practise.** You know when you see a top level presenter on a stage, or on television, and their delivery is just, well, really good? They didn't get there by accident or by winging it. They practised a lot. That means working out what they're going to say, then rehearsing it. Then rehearsing it again.

   Try out your presentation in front of a friendly audience (e.g. a family member). Perhaps try it out in front of a mirror. The more you practise, the better.

2. **Nerves – they're normal!** There is hardly a single speaker I've ever spoken to that doesn't feel at least some nerves before they speak. In fact, I'd go so far as to say that it would be a bad thing if you didn't feel a bit nervous. The good news is that, over time, signs of nerves will disappear.

An easy tip to cut out one sign of nerves is if you are using notes, put the paper down on the table in front of you. If you are holding the paper, then there is the tendency for the paper to flap around as nerves make your hands shake.

3. **Notes.** On the subject of notes, there is absolutely no need to feel that you have to memorise your presentation, especially as you start out. Having said that, definitely don't just read it out.

   Many of us like to have some notes as a crutch to lean on, but it's far better to have them written out as bullet points. This will allow you, if you forget where you are, to look down, check your next point and then carry on.

4. **It doesn't matter if you forget.** No one knows what you're going to say. If you forget a bit of your prepared speech, no one will be any the wiser.

5. **Slow down.** Another sign of nerves when presenting is talking fast. When presenting, if the words sound way too slow to you, the presenter, you're probably speaking at about the right pace for your audience. Less really can be more, so don't try to pack too much content into your presentation.

6. **Breathe.** A good way of reducing nerves is to work on your breathing just before you present. Andy Bounds shared this tip with me, and it has served me very well. It is called 1-4-2 breathing: this involves inhaling

(one second), holding the breath (four seconds), and exhaling (two seconds).

Do this in ratio: I tend to go with 2-8-4. Repeat this 10 times before speaking, and the increased oxygen flowing round the body will help you feel more confident.

7. **Vary tone and volume.** Sometimes you hear presentations where the speaker just talks in a monotone voice. How boring is that? Don't inflict the same pain on your audience. Talking loudly or quietly can help emphasise a point. A brief period of silence will make sure your audience is listening. Varying your tone of voice also helps keep your audience interested in what you're saying.

8. **Eye contact.** We've already discussed how important it is for your audience to feel engaged in your presentation. Clearly, the content will have a big role to play in this, but don't discount your eye contact with your audience. This will depend on how many people are listening to you, but try to cast your eyes around your audience as you speak, such that you get full eye contact with everyone for a second or two. Do this, and they'll be engaged in what you're saying.

As an audience member, when you get eye contact with the speaker, it feels like they are talking to you personally, which means you listen more. Just be careful not to stare at people: this will freak them out!

9. **Don't go on.**   Respect your audience by finishing your presentation on time. If you don't, you'll either be cutting into the next presenter's time, which is disrespectful, or you'll get timed out. In the latter case, this will make it look like you haven't prepared. When we're trying to get over how good our business is, this doesn't help!

10. **Don't worry!** I'll finish this section by talking as one Unnatural Networker to another. Presenting can be a nerve-wracking activity, when we have already put ourselves out of our comfort zone simply by being there. But the best advice I can give is to not worry.

    Everyone else in the room is another business owner, and we're all on the same side. I promise you, they are all willing you to do well, so just try to relax and enjoy it.

Chapter 10 Action Points

- Write your presentation using the template on Pages 177-178. Start with your ask – who is your top target?

- Think of a story of an existing client that illustrates why your target would want to speak to you.

- Prepare a one-page document with the key bullet points of your presentation.

- Practise. Practise as much as possible. Deliver the presentation to a friend/colleague/family member to get their feedback.

- If you're in a networking group, prepare more presentations so you have a different one for every meeting.

PART 4

After the
Networking Event

Let's look at what we've achieved so far.

We've been out networking! Not only that, we've been to different types of events, both casual contact and strong contact.

We've met new people, we've built better relationships over a one-to-one, and we've also learned how to present our business to a networking audience.

But there's one last part of this book still to come. We've got to think about what we do when we leave whichever networking event we've been to. What happens when we get back home/to the office? So in Chapter 11, we'll discuss networking follow up.

While we're in the comfort of our own premises, we'll have the chance to network online, so we'll cover that in Chapter 12.

Lastly, in Chapter 13, we'll look at how we can devise our networking strategy, as you, the Unnatural Networker, look to put into practice what you've learned.

CHAPTER 11

Follow Up

Recently, I attended a big networking event in central London. Given the hundreds of people in attendance, it was a big surprise to bump into Chris, my old boss. I was keen to catch up with him, but I wanted to meet other people, and it was also so busy you could hardly hear yourself speak.

So a few days later, we met for coffee so we could catch up on the gossip. More importantly though, it turned out that we were both in a position to help each other. I was really excited; his current role was on a project with a client that I'd been interested to get an introduction to, and I'd done some work with a company that Chris's firm really wanted to pitch to.

As the one-to-one meeting progressed, I took copious notes on who Chris needed to talk to, and the best way of setting up the meeting. I also knew what I had to say if I got a response of 'Oh, we've already got someone who deals with that for us…' I had all the information I needed to create a strong referred introduction.

We then started to talk about the client Chris was working with, and we went over the same information for me. I told him a story about a particular client of mine, similar to my target, and how we'd managed to increase their sales by 56%.

Later on, I made a priority of setting up the introduction for Chris, so I called my contact. Unfortunately, the company had restructured, and my contact was no longer the person that Chris would need to speak to. However, he said that he'd see what he could do, but warned me that it might take a few weeks. I thanked him, and dropped a quick email to Chris to keep him updated.

I didn't think anything of it when I didn't get a reply to this email, as I'd only seen Chris that day. But I did start to wonder when, three weeks later, I'd not heard from Chris. On that day, I'd called my contact to see if there had been any progress. I was pleased to hear that there was, and they asked if Chris could call the following day. Immediately, I gave Chris a ring to tell him the good news, at which he was naturally delighted.

I then asked whether Chris himself had made any progress on his client. His answer, however, was very vague. He mumbled a bit about how he'd been really busy recently, and it had simply slipped his mind.

I remembered back to our meeting: whereas I'd taken notes on how to make Chris's introduction, he had not written down a single thing about how to help me. I hadn't really thought about it at the time, but thinking about it now, it did seem a bit strange given the nature of our conversation at the time. I then remembered the email that he hadn't replied to, and then it all started to make sense. Chris just wasn't very good at following up.

So I asked him straight: it turned out he had forgotten a couple of details that we'd talked about, and, embarrassed, hadn't called me to check. He told me he'd put a call in straightaway, and fortunately I got the opportunity to speak to his client.

Now, as it all turned out well in the end, it's very easy to just forget this and move on. But consider for a second what would have happened if I hadn't challenged Chris about why he hadn't spoken to his client? I would never have had the opportunity that I did. Equally, what if he'd just jotted down a few notes when we had the one-to-one? I might have got in front of my new client much sooner!

What is follow up?

The short answer is that follow up makes everything else we've been discussing so far in this book worthwhile. Without it, every Unnatural Networker comfort zone you've stepped out of, every action you've taken, every person you've met, every business card you've given out: all of that will have been a complete waste of time.

Think about the following scenarios:

> 1. *You got chatting with a business person at a mixer networking event. There was some common ground between your two businesses, and you agreed when chatting that it would definitely be a good idea to meet up for a coffee.*

> 2. *You delivered a great 60 second presentation on your business, telling an excellent story about how you helped one of your clients. Someone came up to you afterwards, told you how interested they were in what you'd said, and gave you their business card saying 'call me'.*

3. In a conversation with someone after a networking meeting, they show an interest in your business, so you promise to email them over some information about your latest offers.

4. In a one-to-one meeting, it becomes clear that you have a client that your fellow networker would be keen to be introduced to. You have enough credibility with the client in question, so you agree to introduce them.

5. After your weekly networking group meeting, one of the members tells you that they know someone that could introduce you to your dream client. All they'd need from you is to know how to start a conversation about you, so you agree to have a phone call to move things forward.

In each case, the action required is fairly simple. It's either sending an email, or making a phone call. Follow up is completing this action (and of course any further actions that result).

But what would happen if you didn't complete the simple follow up action?

Why is follow up so important?

To answer this question, let's remind ourselves of a concept we first discussed in Chapter 3 – the VCP process.

The VCP© Process

What VCP tells us is that when we're networking, we hope to set up a profitable relationship with our fellow networker, but to get to P we need to go through V and C first. V is for Visibility: we meet someone, we get to know them and their business. C, or Credibility, is where we get to find out if someone is any good.

When it comes to follow up, we are still very much in the visibility stage. Follow up is the first test of credibility. At this point, we're not actually being judged on the technical part of what we do (i.e. are we a good *accountant*?). This is really a test to see what sort of person we are: and in that I believe we can find the true definition of follow up.

Follow up is doing what you say you're going to do, nothing more. If you say you're going to send an email, send it! If you say you'll call to set up a time to have a coffee, make the call! If you say you're going to make an introduction, make it!

So, what would happen if you didn't complete the follow up action in each of the scenarios above? The answer is your credibility will suffer, meaning you have less chance of reaching a state of profitability with each of the people involved. Each one of those situations suggests an opportunity for your business: you'd be mad not to complete the follow up!

But, bizarrely, experience shows that many people don't follow up after networking. It could be for a number of reasons. Chris, in the story above, felt embarrassed that he didn't know every detail that he needed to know. It could be that people over-promise when in a networking situation. It could be that people simply don't understand the importance of follow up and the damage that is done to their credibility.

Whatever it is though, it does give us Unnatural Networkers an opportunity. Hopefully it is becoming clear that following up isn't difficult. It is just incumbent upon us to do what we say we are going to do. It is therefore very easy for us to move upwards in the VCP process and establish our credibility, just by following up well.

Not only that, but because we are more likely to have been a little more introverted in our conversations, and perhaps not spoken to quite as many people when we're out networking, the chances are we've got less follow up to forget about or get wrong.

How important is follow up to other networkers?

BNI, as an organisation of over 150,000 networkers worldwide, has done a number of surveys over time that look at various aspects of networking. One question that is frequently asked is: 'What character traits do great networkers possess?' The same answer has come up time and again: the number one trait of good networkers is that they follow up effectively.

Let's just consider what this fact tells us for a moment. Remember, this information is coming from BNI members, people who network regularly and who receive networking training. What they see consistently is people failing to follow up, which, as we've seen, totally negates any time and effort put in. It is so easy to get ahead in networking, even for Unnatural Networkers: just make sure your credibility is sky high by following up well.

How to follow up

OK. Hopefully we're on the same page here: follow up is important. Let's now have a closer look at HOW we can follow up as effectively as possible. To do that, I'd like to tell you a quick story.

The story is about one of the early networking functions I attended. It was a Chamber of Commerce meeting in Greenwich in south-east London, and I partly remember that day because it was absolutely pouring with rain (which will become relevant as you'll see).

The meeting overall was a success. I'd set myself a goal of the number of people I wanted to meet, pushed myself out of my comfort zone to go and meet them, and during the process of the lunch meeting, collected a bunch of business cards. Of these, five had a specific follow up action, while the remainder I would add to my database.

It then came to the time to leave, and as I walked outside, I stepped into the aforementioned rain. Not having an umbrella with me, I had to run as fast as I could to my car. Despite only being in the rain for less than two minutes, I was soaked through by the time I opened my car door, such that temporarily I completely forgot about the stack of business cards in my pocket.

I drove back to my office, thinking that once I got there, I'd start my follow up then. I put the pile of business cards on my desk, right next to the phone, ready for action.

However, at this point my everyday world took over. I'm sure you know what I mean: you've been away from your workplace for a few hours, and the emails go crazy and suddenly the phone doesn't stop ringing. I really had intended to get straight on with the follow up but, all of a sudden, the whole of the rest of the day had passed me by, and I'd done nothing. I'd get on with the follow up tomorrow.

The next morning arrived; I looked at the pile of cards again, and thought to myself *I must follow up with those contacts today, it's important.* But then whatever was urgent that day took precedence, and the cards didn't get looked at.

A day or two later, I started to feel a bit guilty about not calling the relevant people, but I couldn't honestly remember what I needed to do with each of the cards.

So I moved the cards to the special place on my desk for important matters: the top drawer. There, forgotten about, they stayed until I cleared out my desk some months later.

So, what can we learn from this? Well, firstly I'd like to think that I've learned a lot about follow up since then! But that story helps illustrate three key points that will help you follow up effectively every time:

1. Use a memory jogger

I don't know about you, but alongside being an Unnatural Networker, I also have a memory like a sieve. My old boss, Chris (the one in the story above), used to fire out instructions, and unless I wrote them down in detail, I'd always find myself two minutes later thinking *I'm sure he asked me to do something else…*

Even if you've got a good memory, when you go to a networking event and meet 10 people, it isn't easy to remember 10 different pieces of follow up action.

> *Met @ Chamber event 14/3*
>
> *– Has contacts at Barclays/Natwest*
>
> *– Call Monday to set up 1-1*

There's a very simple solution. When you are chatting to someone, as soon as you've agreed whatever follow up is required, ask for their business card and make a brief note on it. Some people even leave a space for notes in their business card design. It doesn't half make it easier to remember what follow up needs to be done:, whether it is 'connect on LinkedIn', or 'phone to arrange one-to-one'.

Writing is an important part of the way visual learners take in information. 70% of the world's population are, to a greater or lesser extent, visual learners. When you follow up, you'll see their card, with their name and details on it in your writing, and this will trigger you into action to call them to follow up.

Incidentally, I always ask the person's permission to write on their card. This isn't strictly necessary, but it is a habit that I've got into. For most people, it is a non-issue, but for some, you can tell by the look on their face that they appreciated being asked. It's just a small step in the relationship-building process…

2. When should follow up start?

The rain that day in Greenwich didn't help with my follow up, but it did teach me a valuable lesson. I've heard networking specialists tell me that there is a huge amount of value in the business cards that you collect. Quite frankly though, if the pile of cards just gets shuffled around your desk, they are worth absolutely nothing.

If there is going to be some value attached to those cards, action needs to happen sooner, and certainly before distractions arise. Ever since that Greenwich meeting, I've made a rule for myself.

I start my follow up as soon as I leave the event I'm at. This may be in my car before I drive away, on the train on the way back, or when I get back to the office before I switch on my laptop. I may even find a quiet corner of the room where the event is taking place.

Whichever it is, just taking a quick look through the stack of business cards with notes on makes such a difference to remembering what needs to happen.

I usually divide the cards into two piles: one for cards needing definitive and important action, the other for general contacts that I will add to my database. Sometimes, there's a third pile: it's for those cards that have been forced upon me at the event!

What to do with all those business cards...

This is an important question, because if you're out networking regularly you will collect a lot of business cards. If the pile of collected business cards isn't going to become unmanageable, working out a system to use them effectively is important.

There are apps available that scan business cards and add them straight into your contacts list on your mobile.

For some this works very well. I don't find this practical because I find my contacts list becomes unwieldy.

Another option is to connect with your new contacts on social media, particularly on LinkedIn. We'll discuss online networking in much more detail in Chapter 12, but here's one suggestion that will make it far more likely for the person you're connecting with to connect back with you.

LinkedIn has a generic connection script that is sent through their in-mail system:

✉ Invite **Mark** to connect on linkedIn

How do you know Mark?

- ⊙ Colleague
- ⊙ Classmate
- ⊙ We've done business together
- ⊙ Friend
- ⊙ Other
- ⊙ I don't know Mark

Include a personal note: (optional)

I'd like to add you to my professional network on LinkedIn

- Charlie Lawson

Important: Only invite people you know well and who know you. Find out why.

[Send Invitation] or Cancel

How personal does that look? Not at all!

Remember, the person you're connecting with will have met a number of other people at the event. They won't necessarily remember you (that may depend on how quickly, or if, they do THEIR follow up!)

Instead, how about the following:

✉ Invite **Mark** to connect on linkedIn

How do you know Mark?

- ◯ Colleague
- ◯ Classmate
- ◯ We've done business together
- ◯ Friend
- ◯ Other
- ◯ I don't know Mark

Include a personal note: (optional)

Hi Mark,

Great to meet you yesterday at the Chamber of Commerce meeting. In advance of our follow up meeting next week, I thought we should also connect on LinkedIn.

See you next Wednesday.

- Charlie Lawson

Important: Only invite people you know well and who know you. Find out why.

[Send Invitation] or Cancel

A personal message like this will definitely increase the chance of them connecting back. It makes it look much more like you actually want to build a relationship.

The third option is to use a business card holder of some kind. I include this because in a networking group, there is a genuine way to ensure that business cards DO hold some real value. For example, in BNI, members are trained to carry around the cards of all the members, and to look for business opportunities for them.

A word of warning...

It is very tempting, on receiving a stack of business cards, to add all the new contact details on to the mailing list for your newsletter and special offer emails. The amount of spam email all of us clear out from our inbox every day is frightening. Nothing says hard sell and 'I don't want to build a relationship with you' more than spam emails. No one wants it, so don't do it. Rant over.

Follow up is always vital

Throughout this chapter, we've covered following up after a networking event. However, remember that the principles we've discussed apply equally across other forms of networking. After a one-to-one meeting, there will be follow up. You won't have room for your notes on the back of a business card, but you'll almost certainly need to remind yourself of actions agreed.

Similarly, after a networking group meeting, there will be actions to complete. Perhaps there are referral requests to follow up on, or potential visitors to invite. Doing that follow up immediately while it is fresh in the mind is by far the most productive way to get things done.

Get to it!

Chapter 11 Action Points

- At your next networking event, write follow up notes on the back of the business cards of people you meet.

- Look through the business cards you've collected before you leave the event to work out what follow up is required. At the very latest, do this on the way back.

- Do whatever follow up action you agreed upon!

- Add your new contacts to your database so you can reconnect with them in the future.

- Personalise the generic contact request script given on online platforms when you connect with people you've met.

CHAPTER 12

Online Networking

Throughout this book we've focused on face to face networking. It's now time to explore what's happening online.

Online networking just cannot be ignored, especially in an internet-driven world. However, there's great news: as an Unnatural Networker, there are some major advantages to online networking. These allow us to stay well within our comfort zone.

Benefits of online networking

1. **Wider pool of contacts**: compared to face to face networking, it is possible to reach a far wider audience online. Even if you go to a large networking event, for example with 1,000 attendees, two challenges present themselves. Firstly, it won't ever be possible to meet all of the attendees. Secondly, that was just one event; 1,000 is a lot of people, but in the context of the world, or this country, or even (in most cases) the town you live in, 1,000 isn't many.

   Online networking allows you to network with other people all over the world!

2. **Easy to find people**: you may think that given this extraordinary number of people to network with, it would be hard to find the right people. Think again. It is really easy to search for the right contacts and conversations online. Take our large face to face networking event with 1,000 attendees. Let's also assume that you are interested in meeting web

designers; on the delegate list, there are 30 web designers present. There is a lot of filtering to do to meet the right people.

Online meanwhile, it is a very simple process to search for web designers. You can also search for contacts by location. Almost immediately, you can be networking with the type of people who you want to network with.

3. **From the comfort of your own home**: that's right, Unnatural Networkers, you can network online in your own home or office. You don't have to venture out, you don't have to actually speak to anyone. Hey, you can even network online wearing your pyjamas…

4. **Time and cost savings**: apart from an internet connection, and the time you spend, online networking tends to be free. When networking face to face, you'll need to travel to and from the events you attend, while there will likely be a meeting fee as well.

5. **Efficiency**: because you are networking in your own premises, it is likely that you'll have everything you need. For example, if a networking contact asks a question of you, you'll have the resources to answer straightaway. Providing quick and accurate responses is a great way to build credibility.

6. **Positioning yourself as an expert**: it is very easy to do this online. You just have to share good content in your area of expertise. Because online networking is searchable, people can find your content. We'll look at this in greater detail shortly.

It's all networking...

Despite all this, many people still believe that online networking is a waste of time. I've lost count of the number of times that I've heard business professionals saying things like:

> 'All I ever get online is hard sell spam from people I don't care about.'

> 'I'm sick and tired of getting contact requests from people I don't know.'

> 'I just don't care what someone is having for their lunch.'

Let's take each of these phrases in turn, to see if we can understand the problems that we face when networking online.

'All I ever get online is hard sell spam from people I don't care about.'

Xxxxxxx Xxxxxxx   7m
Bargain of a sale on these polka meeting chairs: ow.ly/vNCgv £55+VAT each reduced from £75+VAT

Expand   Reply   Retweet   ★ Favorite   Buffer   ••• More

Well, you know what, if online networking was JUST hard selling, it wouldn't be much fun. Think back to Chapter 2, when we looked at the definition of networking. I shared a story about a man who tried to hard sell his combined domestic fire and security system to me. That was face to face hard sell, and didn't get him any sales.

Hard selling online does happen, but it will yield the same results. So don't do it! Networking is about building relationships, whether you're face to face or online. The principle doesn't change.

'I'm sick and tired of getting contact requests from people I don't know.'

> On 03/11/14 2.50PM, James Sxxxxxx wrote:
> ---------------------
> I'd like to add you to my professional network on LinkedIn

To help answer this frustration, let me share a quick story. I was chatting with a fellow Unnatural Networker recently about online networking. He said he was getting really frustrated with LinkedIn.

He understood that it was important that he had a presence on the network, but found himself inundated with connection requests. Plenty of them were from people he didn't know. I asked him what he did with all these requests: he simply clicked 'ignore'.

We then started talking about the face to face networking meeting where we'd first met. What had he been thinking when I had approached him and introduced myself? He said that he was delighted to have a conversation, as he was feeling slightly lost.

Given that we go to networking events to meet new people, it is highly unlikely any businessperson would deliberately ignore someone at a networking event. So why do it online?

Networking is networking, whether it is offline or online. It is all about building relationships. Sometimes those relationships lead to something. Sometimes they don't. Having met someone face to face, if the relationship goes 'wrong' in some way, you simply don't see that person any more. Likewise online: it is very easy to disconnect with contacts on LinkedIn if necessary.

The key to accepting contact requests is to then do something about them. Will you build a relationship through online conversation, or arrange to meet for a one-to-one?

Remember: once upon a time, you didn't know your best current client. Who's to say that people connecting with you won't become a client? Who's to say they don't know someone who'll become your best client?

'I just don't care what someone is having for their lunch.'

You and me both! Who really cares, especially if we don't know the person? There is so much irrelevant content on social media, and it takes time to wade through it.

However, judicious use of the various search facilities available in social media makes it far easier to find the relevant content that is of interest.

Perhaps the best example of this is the use of hashtags. A hashtag is where a word (or phrase but with no spaces between the words) is preceded by the # symbol. The practice started out in Twitter, but has spread to other social networks.

So, for example, if you're interested in finding people talking about web design, you could enter the hashtag #webdesign into Twitter's search function, and it would bring up a list of tweets containing the hashtag. From there, you can find relevant content.

Not only that, you can see who is sharing this content. Connect with them, and you'll start to receive the content that you want, as opposed to the morass of general information that people are posting.

Picking the right social network

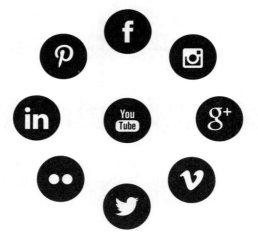

I need to hold my hands up here right now. I'm not expert enough in any of the social networks to be writing about them in detail, so I'm not going to do that. However, I can give you a take on where is the best place for you in terms of getting results from your online networking.

Case Study – Me:

As you can probably imagine, as an Unnatural Networker, I didn't participate in online networking. This continued until September 2011, when BNI as an organisation started focusing on its social presence online. It became clear then that I had to do something about my own presence!

I soon realised how much there was to learn. It also became clear that all of the networks were very different, and there needed to be different approaches to each one. After that, something became very obvious, and I kept getting the same advice. What I learned was that there is a social network for everyone. You just have to find the right social network for you.

One of my biggest challenges in business is replying to emails. It often takes me a lot of time to phrase my reply. I'll think *Is there a better way to say this?* or *How will the recipient read it?* The same challenge presented itself within social media, such as when responding to contacts on LinkedIn or to messages on Facebook.

That's why, for me at least, Twitter is brilliant. You've only got 140 characters, which means I can't spend too long agonising over responses. It also doesn't take too much time to stay in touch with lots of contacts. So, it's definitely Twitter for me.

There are three main networks online that you, as a business user, should be considering. Those three are LinkedIn, Twitter and Facebook. That is by no means an exhaustive list; there are plenty of others (think Google +, Instagram, Pinterest and many more). By the time you read this, more will doubtless have been created.

In addition, some of the bigger networks often have their own social networking tool that is built in as part of membership. For example, BNI's system, BNI Connect, allows BNI members to connect in any part of the world.

In her book *The FT Guide to Business Networking*, Heather Townsend has a brilliant analogy to give you an idea of what LinkedIn, Twitter and Facebook are, and more importantly, how you should use them.

She says that LinkedIn is very much like being at work. It is a forum to discuss professional or business issues. While relationship-building is still of course important, business is most definitely the focus.

Meanwhile, Heather argues that Twitter is very much like a cocktail party. There will be lots of different people there, all chatting away about various topics. Personality comes into the equation more than in LinkedIn. For example, at a real cocktail party, there will likely be a lot of relationship-building 'chit chat', and Twitter is just the same.

In comparison to the other two, Facebook is very much a social network. Heather contends that it is a place to let your hair down at the end of the day. Typically, users are interested in social content: photos, gossip and such like. That's not to say, however, that there isn't a business context to these sorts of conversations.

From my experience, Heather's analogy is spot on. Each of the networks has a slightly different approach, and what works on one won't necessarily work on another. However, there are some similarities between them too.

Your profile

All social networks will require you to set up a personal profile so that other users can see who you are and decide whether they want to connect with you. This broadly translates in the face to face networking world to meeting someone in the flesh, finding out about them briefly, and getting their business card.

Generally, the more information you provide, the better. Crucially though, make sure you include a photo.

 or  ?

This is vital: the analogy I'd draw here would be to think about online dating. No one would ever go on a date with someone without seeing a photo! While we're not planning to go out with people we meet on social media, the same principle applies. When picking a photo to put on your profile, use a head and shoulders shot. They come up so small that anything else makes it very hard to see who is in the photo.

Don't forget: your profile will change depending on what network you're on. LinkedIn will be far more professional, and will read like a CV. Facebook meanwhile will be far more personal: your picture might be a recent holiday snap. However, you may equally decide to pick one picture that is suitable across all formats, because you'll start to generate a more recognisable brand.

Hide in the Shadows?

Should your profile focus on you as a person, or on your company? You'll see this on Twitter a lot: all you can see is a company name and logo in the picture. I can certainly appreciate that as an Unnatural Networker, it is tempting to hide yourself behind your company logo.

But I would urge you to step out from the shadows. At the very least, have a personal profile and a separate company one too. As we've seen time and again throughout this book, networking is about building relationships. We do business with people, we build relationships with people. So make sure your name and picture are prominent as well as your company's name.

Contacts

As we've already seen, online networking allows you to access a huge number of people. A key metric for anyone on social media is the number of contacts that you have. However, as we'll come to see, it's less about the overall number of contacts you have; more important is the quality of the relationships you have. That's what will get you the best returns.

Having contacts is important though, and the only real difference is how they are termed. On LinkedIn they're called 'Connections', on Facebook they are 'Friends', and on Twitter they are known as 'Followers'.

How do you develop your list of contacts?

Sharing content

Well, one part of the answer to that comes straightaway. Sharing good content that people are interested in is a fundamental plank of online networking. This content largely comes in the form of links to web-based material. This means that the whole video or article won't appear (clearly, in Twitter that would be impossible with only 140 characters to play with).

If you share content that people want, whether that's by reading it, hearing it, looking at it, or viewing it, you'll start to develop a following.

As an Unnatural Networker, the key is to understand two key facts. Firstly, in the digital world, there is literally something for everybody. One of the great things that the internet has done for the world is to provide the ability to search for anything. This means that someone out there is also interested in what you're interested in.

Secondly, what you do IS interesting. Not all Unnatural Networkers realise this. There will, absolutely guaranteed, be people out there that have an interest in what you do and what you say.

Case Study: Content is out there, being consumed!

I had a conversation recently about LinkedIn with Emily, a particularly Unnatural Networker. She runs a lettings company, and was incredulous at the thought that anyone might want to read her thoughts on her business and her industry.

To help prove my point, I asked her what she was interested in outside work. Emily was into horse riding. I asked whether she'd ever looked up horse riding on LinkedIn: never! Imagine her surprise then, when a quick search in LinkedIn groups revealed over 70 dedicated groups discussing horse riding.

For Emily, simply realising what is out there was a crucial step in taking the decision to open up to online networking.

What content can you share and how do you do it? One of the best ways to share content is through the process of blogging. A blog is a short article that appears online, taking the form of a written blog, a video blog or an audio blog.

This isn't the place to go into the technicalities of how to blog. But whether you set up your own dedicated blog site, or add a section to your website, or simply add some videos to your homepage: get going. Written blogs don't have to be long: a side of A4 or up to 500 words is plenty.

If the thought of creating a video is too expensive (not to mention nerve-wracking), or writing just isn't your thing, there is another option. You can share content by re-posting information that you like. The most obvious form of this is on Twitter, where content commonly gets re-tweeted (look for 'RT' at the beginning of the tweet).

If I read an article that I find interesting, then I want my followers to have the chance to see the same content:

The best bit about sharing content is that it gives you the ability to position yourself easily as an expert in your field. As we saw earlier in the chapter, being able to search for content by keyword or hashtag makes it very easy for users to search for information that is interesting to them. If you're creating this high-quality content, users will find you and connect with you. This will also happen when sharing other people's content too, but of course to a lesser extent.

Engagement

So sharing content helps you generate contacts. But there's another, easier way too. Let's not forget: online networking is networking, and we know what that means. It's all about building relationships.

So a very quick way to build your contact list online is to start to interact with people. If someone poses a question, answer it. If someone replies to one of your posts, reply back. If someone posts a reply in your blog, respond. If someone connects with you, say hello. This really isn't rocket science; all you have to do is reply. You never know where the relationship might lead you.

Another place where you can engage online is on LinkedIn, in the groups functionality. You can search for relevant content in topic-specific groups. In each group there will be a number of discussion threads. By engaging within these communities, you will increase your exposure and attract new contacts.

How to make online networking really work

I was out for a drink with an old school friend recently, and he asked me a question. "You know that networking thing you do, isn't it becoming more and more irrelevant given the rise of social media?"

It's an interesting question. For years, networking has been all about meeting up face to face. As we've seen throughout this book, we build relationships with our networking contacts, and over the course of time we develop those relationships into profitable ones.

However, what's the point of spending time and effort doing that, my friend was intimating, when it is so easy to reach a far wider audience online? Surely building relationships with people face to face isn't the most effective use of time in the modern day and age.

The thing is, to a certain extent, he is absolutely right. It is of course much easier to reach a wider pool of contacts online. But building up connections is only the start of the process. This will help increase your visibility to a wider audience, but you can't then just jump straight into profitability.

Credibility must come first. While it is certainly possible to build credibility online, it is much better achieved face to face. This is because face to face networking makes it so much easier to create the depth of relationship required to truly generate credibility.

Think about it. When you sit down for a coffee with another businessperson, and ask them about their business, you find out far more than you will by browsing through their various online profiles.

The best strategy, then, is to combine your networking efforts. Firstly, create a wide network by going online; this takes advantage of the key benefit of the wider pool of potential contacts. Then you need to move on to create the necessary depth of relationships by networking face to face.

Ignore online or face to face and you'll be missing out. It will either take longer to increase your visibility, or you won't generate enough credibility to make your networking profitable.

That's why I raised the point earlier in this chapter about the perceived value of having a big following on social media. Take a quick look around Twitter for example, and you'll see huge numbers of people who are only looking to grow their follower count.

The perception is that more followers means being 'better' at social media. But I heartily disagree. As with anything in business, if there aren't returns to be made, what's the point? Having a vast number of connections is useless if none of them do business with you or refer you.

So, a successful online networking strategy involves the following:

- Working out which networks would be most appropriate for your business, and crucially, you.

- Generating connections, whether you go looking for them or vice versa.

- Sharing good quality content to demonstrate your expertise and credibility.

- Engaging with your connections to start the process of building a relationship.

- Moving to a face to face setting once you're ready to take the relationship forward. This is exactly the same process as following up (Chapter 11).

But this is all too much!

It would be very easy for us, as Unnatural Networkers, to consider online networking as just another item in an already hectic business schedule. How on earth are we going to find the time to add social media activity into our working week, especially when we have to take the time to learn it in the first place?

All I can say is that I know exactly how you feel, and I'd like to remind you of my social media story. Remember, I'm an Unnatural Networker just like you. Maybe, because I'm not a social media 'expert', my take on the subject is that bit more relevant to you.

A little over two years ago, I felt exactly the same as you do now. I couldn't work out the various networks, and I didn't understand what I was doing with them. Most of all, I couldn't see how I could fit online networking into my diary.

But what I've found is that I now have at my fingertips a tool that has allowed me to vastly increase my network. It allows me not only to communicate with my clients (i.e. BNI members), but also has cemented my position as a networking expert.

There's no way I would have written this book had it not been for social media.

To help you get around these obstacles, here are some key learnings that I've discovered over the last couple of years:

1.	**Aim low!**	There's no point attempting to change the world in one fell swoop. It simply won't happen. Decide which of the online networks is most appropriate for you, and try that one first.
2.	**Little and often**	It's much better to succeed in posting online once a week than aiming for five times a day and failing. Consistency is key.
3.	**Keep at it!**	With point 2 in mind, ensure that your account doesn't lie dormant. What you post online will be in cyberspace forever. Finding accounts lying unused is a big credibility killer.
4.	**Use an app called Buffer**	Seriously, this was the tool that made it possible for me to get going on social media. Buffer links with one or more of your social media accounts, and you then queue up posts in your 'buffer' which are then sent out in predetermined timeslots. Buffer is free (for low usage which is plenty to get you going). Using Buffer also ensures you cover point 2: all you need to do is diarise ten minutes a week to get your posts queued up.

5.	Be careful!	Social media can be very addictive! It is all too easy to spend too much time on it. Recognise upfront that your timeline will contain reams of complete rubbish from people you don't know. The key is to filter through the irrelevant material, and focus on what is relevant to you.
6.	There's a social network for everyone!	I do firmly believe that some networks are more suited to some people than others. As I've outlined, I'm definitely a Twitter man. That won't necessarily change, but I have been getting more and more interested in Facebook lately...

Chapter 12 Action Points

- Open your mind to the power of social media. It isn't a fad that will go away, it is part of life in the 21st century! Google 'Social Media Revolution' for a great video detailing why.

- Pick which online network is most suitable for you.

- Set up a profile, including a good quality headshot.

- Search for contacts to connect with/follow. Use a hashtag relevant to your industry (e.g. #webdesign) to find people.

- Use Buffer to queue up posts on your chosen network. These could be your own blog articles, or retweets/ shares of content from other people.

- Reply back when you are contacted!

CHAPTER 13

Developing a
Networking Strategy

So that's it. We've covered everything you need to know to transform yourself from a non-networker to an Unnatural Networker. Perhaps you've even moved yourself into the networking comfort zone.

We've looked at what networking you can do and how to approach strangers. We've started and maintained conversations, and presented our business. We've also looked at following up properly so that your credibility soars, and how to network online.

However, if seeing a genuine return for your business is important, you can't just rush into networking without considering the best approach for you. Everyone is different. The key thing is to work out the right strategy for you, and then stick to it.

Here's what to think about when putting your strategy together:

Where is best for you to network?

We looked in detail at the various types of network in Chapter 4, but as a reminder, different networks suit different purposes. If you are just interested in making some contacts, then a casual contact network will work well for you.

If you are looking to generate referrals, then a strong contact network would be best. However, if your business has you flying around the world most weeks, then you would never be able to maintain the commitment required to get the most out of the group. Service clubs, industry networks, and women only networks all have their pros and cons, while of course there is the huge potential of the online networking world.

The best networkers (who may well be Unnatural Networkers) tend to choose two or three networks. You're not then putting all your eggs in one basket, nor spreading yourself too thinly. This leads us neatly on to...

Only commit to what you can

It's not worth trying to network in too many places or groups. When will you get any actual work done?! We're not going to be in business long if we don't serve our clients. Secondly, and more importantly, is the fact that there are only so many relationships that you're going to be able to maintain at a time.

In Chapter 12 on online networking, we discussed the width and depth of your network. Your network can only get so wide before the quality of relationships will inevitably suffer. You'll be too busy to keep up with your contacts, or you'll start missing networking events, which will damage both your visibility and credibility.

So as you develop your first networking strategy, the best suggestion I can give is to start slowly. Work on developing consistency to your networking. If that means networking once a month, go for that while you practise. Once up to speed, network more regularly. In terms of results, little and often is so much better than lots and sometimes, so pick one network and work it properly.

Get your diary out

Networking requires commitment (another reason for only committing to what you can). For myself, I've found that the key to committing to networking is to make sure that networking activities are diarised. This is crucial, because once appointments are in the diary, then business people don't usually break them. This includes putting preparation time in the diary.

For example, I would recommend to any networking group member that they put an hour a week in their diary every week. Then they can make sure they've practised their 60-second presentation, and thought about any referrals or visitors to bring to the meeting that week.

It's not just about finding NEW clients

If we are serious about the relationship-building process, then we need to make sure that our networking includes time not only to meet new people, but to maintain contact with existing connections.

But sitting down for a one-to-one with a networking contact will pay dividends. So when planning your time in your diary for networking, make sure you include catching up with your existing contacts.

Just as it is easier to keep existing clients than to find new ones, think about leveraging the relationships that you already have.

Know what you want

The best way to leverage the relationships that you already have is to know who you're after. We saw in Chapter 9 how important it is to be specific when networking.

So a key part of your strategy needs to include developing and maintaining a top ten list of dream clients. If you don't know who you want to speak to, how will anyone else? Not only that, but make sure you have a think about which stories you'd tell to make sure you can back up your referral requests.

Plan to help others

We've seen time and again how important relationships are to networking. So your strategy must include time to work on relationships. The best way to do this is to help others as we saw in Chapter 2 when we discussed Givers Gain.

So, find time to look for creator referrals. Find time to have one-to-ones where you focus solely on the other person's business. Find time to look through your online contacts to generate potential referrals.

If you keep helping other people, giving without expectation, it will come back to you in spades.

Track your return on investment (ROI) – what is networking worth to you?

If we're going to spend business time building relationships, there must be a return from that time invested. If you are not getting a return on your investment, then it is not a sensible commercial decision to devote time to networking.

So, how do you know what your networking is worth to you? You've got to track it.

One thing to bear in mind here is that different networks offer different returns. For example, being part of a casual contact network such as the Chamber of Commerce may not give anything like the return that a strong contact networking group like BNI will.

Equally, you may have joined networks for other reasons. Maybe you're after access to resources and contacts, or for information in an industry-specific network. In these cases, the return may not be in monetary form.

However, whatever you intend to get out your networking, particularly if it is in the form of actual business, it is vital to keep track of what you do generate. It's easy to remember what's happened in the last week or so, but over months and years it becomes harder to track, unless you do something about it. How do you track the business you are generating?

Take recently-retired BNI member Jim Adams, an electrician (his son has now taken over his membership). He'd been in BNI for over six years, and when I asked him how he tracked his networking return, his response genuinely astonished me. He pulled out a slightly battered notepad, and told me that the answer to that question could be found inside.

Slightly puzzled, I flicked through the pages. On every single one, Jim had stuck in BNI referrals he'd received, with meticulous notes on what had happened to each one.

Jim had written down whether the referral had turned into business, and if so how much business it had led to. There were also notes on any follow up required, and whether the referral led to any spin-off business.

As a result, Jim could tell me proudly that BNI had been worth, on average, in excess of £50,000 a year throughout his membership. Naturally, it had grown over time, and there were peaks and troughs. But, as an average, he was very pleased with what he'd received. And I was delighted to hear it!

Jim's notepad got me thinking. How do other networkers track the business they receive through their networking activities? Whether it's via a complicated spreadsheet, or a simple handwritten version like Jim's, I would highly recommend that you look back, and track the business you've generated.

When you do this, you should obviously consider the income generated by direct referrals. Clearly this stems from networking. But I'd also encourage you to think about the spin-off business that you've picked up.

Whenever you write an invoice, consider how that bit of business came to you. Sometimes, the link back to your networking isn't initially clear. But then you remember that the client was introduced to you via person A, you met person A through person B, and you met person B at a networking event. You wouldn't have invoiced that business had you not been to the event that day.

Keep a track of every bit of business you receive; once you get networking, you'll be amazed at how it adds up.

Chapter 13 Action Points

- Choose where you are going to network.

- Only commit to what you can, diarise your networking.

- Make new contacts by talking to people wherever you are.

- Continue to build relationships by reconnecting with people already in your network.

- Go out of your way to help people.

- Work out who your target market is. Once you know, ask for that target specifically!

- Create a spreadsheet to track your returns from networking. If spreadsheets aren't your thing, find another way.

Once an Unnatural Networker, Always an Unnatural Networker

So you've got to the end of this book. Hopefully you've enjoyed it, and most importantly learned something.

As I said way back in Chapter 1, networking is a learned skill. You can teach yourself how to do it. With practice, you will become good at it, and you will start to reap the benefits for your business.

That's about where I find myself now. I'm definitely good at networking, and I see returns for my business through it.

But do I enjoy it? No! Networking still makes me uncomfortable – it still feels Unnatural. I still have to push myself to do it.

So if, having got to this point, you are still feeling a bit of an Unnatural Networker, don't worry. Lots of us 'seasoned' networkers feel the same. You've just got to get out there, remember what you've learned, and go for it.

Good luck!

References

Cain, S. (2012)
Quiet: The Power of Introverts in a World That Can't
Stop Talking.
London, Penguin.

Lopata, A. and Roper, P. (2011)
And Death Came Third!
Hertfordshire, Panoma Press.

Misner, I., Macedonio, M. and Garrison, M. (2006)
Truth or Delusion: Busting Networking's Biggest Myths.
Tennessee, Nelson Books.

Townsend, H. (2011)
FT Guide to Business Networking.
Harlow, Pearson Education.

UCAS (2014)
http://www.ucas.com/
[Accessed on 25 April 2014]

Wikipedia (2014)
http://en.wikipedia.org/wiki/Business_networking
[Accessed on 25 April 2014]

BNI®

BNI is the most successful business networking referral organisation in the world. There are over 13,000 members in the UK and Ireland alone, passing nearly 680,000 referrals worth over £339 million every year! It is quite literally the best way to build a better business.

BNI's philosophy is Givers Gain®, which is simply this: "If I give you business, you'll want to give me business".

BNI allows only one representative from each trade or profession to join any BNI group. This means you can lock out your competition, ensuring you receive 100% of all new business.

BNI teaches its members how to attract and win more new business for each other through word of mouth. Working together, BNI members achieve incredible results, growing their business in ways they could never accomplish alone.

To find your nearest BNI meeting, go to www.bni.co.uk / www.bni.ie.

About the Author

Charlie Lawson is an ardent practitioner of helping businesses to grow, having worked with thousands of business owners over the last 10 years to help them expand their businesses through more effective networking.

He has a passion for seeing business owners succeed. A widely recognised expert on the power of 'word of mouth' marketing, Charlie is a public speaker, trainer and writer on the subject.

Charlie Lawson is the UK & Ireland national director of BNI, the world's largest business networking and referral organisation. Word of mouth referrals accounted for £339 million worth of business passed between BNI members in the UK & Ireland in 2013 – more than 80% of which are B2B SMEs. Charlie's goal is to help BNI members generate £1 billion a year of referral business by 2020.

In any spare time he does have, Charlie enjoys spending time with his partner, Hannah, and running around after his two young children, Alfie and Maggie Mae, as well as wondering if Spurs will ever finish above Arsenal in the league.

Charlie is one inch off a giant and has an inordinately large smile.

Get in touch!

Charlie would love to know how you get on with your networking – let him know! Twitter is the best place to have a chat – find him at @CH_Lawson.

JAICO PUBLISHING HOUSE

Elevate Your Life. Transform Your World.

ESTABLISHED IN 1946, Jaico Publishing House is home to world-transforming authors such as Sri Sri Paramahansa Yogananda, Osho, The Dalai Lama, Sri Sri Ravi Shankar, Robin Sharma, Deepak Chopra, Jack Canfield, Eknath Easwaran, Devdutt Pattanaik, Khushwant Singh, John Maxwell, Brian Tracy and Stephen Hawking.

Our late founder Mr. Jaman Shah first established Jaico as a book distribution company. Sensing that independence was around the corner, he aptly named his company Jaico ('Jai' means victory in Hindi). In order to service the significant demand for affordable books in a developing nation, Mr. Shah initiated Jaico's own publications. Jaico was India's first publisher of paperback books in the English language.

While self-help, religion and philosophy, mind/body/spirit, and business titles form the cornerstone of our non-fiction list, we publish an exciting range of travel, current affairs, biography, and popular science books as well. Our renewed focus on popular fiction is evident in our new titles by a host of fresh young talent from India and abroad. Jaico's recently established Translations Division translates selected English content into nine regional languages.

Jaico's Higher Education Division (HED) is recognized for its student-friendly textbooks in Business Management and Engineering which are in use countrywide.

In addition to being a publisher and distributor of its own titles, Jaico is a major national distributor of books of leading international and Indian publishers. With its headquarters in Mumbai, Jaico has branches and sales offices in Ahmedabad, Bangalore, Bhopal, Bhubaneswar, Chennai, Delhi, Hyderabad, Kolkata and Lucknow.

SINCE 1946